DEVELOPING A TEACHING PORTFOLIO

A GUIDE FOR PRESERVICE AND PRACTICING TEACHERS

Ann Adams Bullock

East Carolina University

Parmalee P. Hawk

East Carolina University

Merrill
Prentice Hall

Upper Saddle River, New Jersey
Columbus, Ohio

Library of Congress Cataloging-in-Publication Data

Adams Bullock, Ann.
    Developing a teaching portfolio : a guide for preservice and practicing teachers / Ann Adams Bullock, Parmalee P. Hawk.
      p. cm.
    Includes bibliographical references and index.
    ISBN 0-13-083040-2
    1. Portfolios in education--United States. 2. Teachers--Rating of--United States. 3. Teachers--Training of--United States. I. Hawk, Parmalee P. II. Title.

LB1728 .A322001
371.14'4--dc21
    00-031859

Vice President and Publisher: Jeffrey W. Johnston
Editor: Debra A. Stollenwerk
Editorial Assistant: Penny S. Burleson
Production Editor: Mary Harlan
Design Coordinator: Diane C. Lorenzo
Cover Design: Diane Ernsberger
Cover Art: SuperStock
Text Design and Illustrations: Carlisle Publishers Services
Production Coordination: Janet Kiefer, Carlisle Publishers Services
Production Manager: Pamela D. Bennett
Director of Marketing: Kevin Flanagan
Market Manager: Amy June
Marketing Services Manager: Krista Groshong

This book was set in Palatino by Carlisle Communication, Ltd. It was printed and bound by R. R. Donnelley & Sons Company. The cover was printed by Phoenix Color Corp.

Photo Credits: All photos by Ann Adams Bullock.

Merrill
Prentice Hall

10 9
ISBN 0-13-083040-2

P R E F A C E

During the past two decades numerous national reports have provoked a wave of reform initiatives that have engulfed the education community. In turn, these initiatives spawn accountability efforts that have focused increased assessment actions upon students and teachers alike. One form of assessment that is enjoying increased popularity, particularly for assessing teacher competence, is the portfolio. *Developing a Teaching Portfolio: A Guide for Preservice and Practicing Teachers* speaks to this form of assessment and concentrates on how teachers can use the portfolio process to demonstrate their competence as professionals.

Developing a Teaching Portfolio can be used in teacher preparation programs, as staff development for practicing teachers to teach the portfolio development process, or for individuals interested in the portfolio process. The book focuses on using portfolios throughout one's professional career. Chapters 1 through 3 are required reading no matter what a teacher's career stage. Chapter 1 provides a brief overview of the accountability and the teacher assessment movements. Chapter 2 defines what a portfolio is and what types of portfolios teachers can develop. Because reflections are the very heart of the portfolio process, Chapter 3 is devoted to the "what, why, when, and how" of writing a reflection. This opening section also addresses legal issues involved with portfolios and with their assessment and scoring.

Chapters 4 through 8 are dedicated to what portfolios should include and how teachers go about developing a portfolio at different stages of their careers. Chapters 4, 5, and 6 center on development of portfolios during the years that teachers are novices. The focus of Chapter 4 is preservice teachers, and Chapter 5 spotlights using the portfolio to obtain employment. Chapter 6 concentrates on preparing a portfolio for continuing licensure. Chapters 7 and 8 are for use by experienced teachers. Chapter 7 suggests using the portfolio as an alternative evaluation process, and Chapter 8 hones in on the master teacher who goes forward for national board certification.

Chapter 9 provides instruction on the use of electronic portfolios at any stage of one's career. This chapter critiques the pros and cons of developing an electronic portfolio and makes suggestions concerning the hardware and software one would use. Our colleagues Drs. David Powers, Scott Thomson, and Kermit Buckner contributed their expertise to this chapter.

ACKNOWLEDGMENTS

In writing this book, we have been influenced by our own experiences as teachers and researchers. In addition, much of our knowledge about portfolios and their development has come from working with more than 300 teachers in elementary, middle, and secondary schools. They have provided us with all the examples in this book (we did not make up the examples) and helped us gather data on portfolio trials, tribulations, and benefits. Therefore, we gratefully acknowledge our debt to the many teachers who permitted us to learn from them and who willingly provided us with reflections, pieces of evidence, and portfolio products. Without them this book would not exist.

A special thanks to Carolyn Smith, Nicole Byrd-Phelps, Kelly Cave, Russell Vernon, Robin Ryder, Carol Brown, and the 1997 and 1998 middle grades majors at East Carolina University. Also, special thanks to Art Bouthillier for the use of his cartoon, "The First Portfolio," and to Scott Thomson for his original cartoons created specifically for this text. To Peggy Hopkins, Mamie Blevins, Kermit Buckner, and Eddie Ingram, we express our appreciation for all the intensive work they have done on North Carolina's Performance-Based Licensure Model for Teachers included in Appendix B. Our "Thank Heaven" Award goes to Sherry Tripp, who made a valiant effort to keep us on track and to keep track of the manuscript.

Our thanks to colleagues who reviewed the manuscript for this handbook: Terry Carson, University of Alberta; Janet Handler, Mount Mercy College; Stephen Lafer, University of Nevada, Reno; Sara Delano Moore, University of Kentucky; Sheryl A. Penn, University of Texas at Tyler; Mike Perl, Kansas State University; and Susan E. Pullman, Youngstown State University.

INTRODUCTION

If you are reading this, you must be interested in creating a portfolio or helping others do so. Congratulations! Portfolios provide an avenue for you, as an educator, to show the depth and breadth of your profession. If this is the first time you have done a portfolio or you have used them for a different purpose than teacher evaluation, this book will provide both the foundation and the specifics to be successful in this endeavor. Readers will find this book easy to read and follow. Information, tips, and examples are provided for teachers at all stages—from those in teacher education programs to those who are interested in national certification. The book is divided into two parts: Chapters 1 through 3 give the background and provide the foundational knowledge of portfolio development, and Chapters 4 through 9 provide specifics and suggestions for teachers and other educators. You should read all of Part One and those chapters in Part Two that match your needs as a portfolio developer.

Chapter 1 gives background information on the reasons and ways portfolios are used for teachers at different stages of their careers. Every reader should begin with this chapter to understand the rationale for portfolio development. Chapter 2 is crucial because it explains the types of portfolios and components of each. Language, terms, and purposes of different portfolios become clear as you read this chapter. For example, the three types of teaching portfolios—process, product, and showcase—are outlined and explained in detail. If you thought there was just one type of portfolio, the information in Chapter 2 should convince you otherwise. Chapter 2 outlines your choices for portfolio development and best options for your situation.

Reflection is considered the most crucial component of portfolio development. Chapter 3 examines the specifics on writing reflections well, followed by examples and sample prompts. Most of you will find the tips for successful writing helpful. In addition, the steps for reflective writing provide detailed instructions and processes to be successful from the first time you try. Overall, the practicality of Chapters 1, 2, and 3 allows you to gather information and resources efficiently since the book is written in simple, nontechnical language.

You should review Part Two of the book (Chapters 4 through 9) before deciding what chapters to focus on. Your purpose for developing portfolios will guide you in deciding which chapter or chapters to read. Each chapter contains the same type of information, but each one has specific components and examples for educators at different career stages. Chapter 4 is written for those of you who are enrolled in a teacher educator program. It gives specific examples and tips for those of you who are expected to create a portfolio as a requirement. If you are creating or redefining a portfolio for a job interview, read

Chapter 5. Tips on defining your portfolio and using it at interviews are highlighted. Chapter 6 is for beginning teachers required to develop portfolios for licensure requirements. Activities, components, and tips for success from teachers are given. An important component of Chapter 6 is the background information about this process. Many times teachers are asked to fulfill requirements and they have no idea why. In this chapter, we outline the important events that lead to this licensure requirement.

Maybe you are an experienced teacher who would like to prepare a portfolio instead of being observed by your administrator for your evaluation. Chapter 7 will give you information for doing this. Several design options are explained and sample assessment criteria are given for the different options. Chapter 8 is for those of you who are interested in becoming nationally board certified. The NBC process, standards, and activities are outlined. You may find the tips from successful candidates most useful. Finally, Chapter 9 gives an overview of an alternative portfolio design—electronic portfolios. Technical information and a comparison of software for this purpose are provided. This chapter gives accurate information about this exciting and innovative approach to portfolio development in light of the current era of technology.

It is our hope that the information in this book will give you the tools and resources to build a portfolio that shows your depth and breadth as an educator. We have enjoyed working with hundreds of teachers who developed portfolios for different reasons at various stages in their career. We hope their experiences and ours, which are evident in these chapters, give you the knowledge and skills needed to create an effective portfolio.

BRIEF CONTENTS

CONTENTS

P A R T I

FOUNDATIONS FOR PORTFOLIO DEVELOPMENT

❧

❧

This book is presented in two parts. The first part, Chapters 1 through 3, is intended for all readers. These chapters present background information and specific details on portfolio development for all teachers and provide the foundation for the second part of the book. Chapter 1 explores the metamorphosis of portfolio development. Chapter 2 gives specific information on how to develop a portfolio. Chapter 3 addresses reflection, the critical component of portfolio development. After reading these three chapters, readers will have the background and information needed to move to the second part of this book. **Please note:** Chapters 1 through 3 are necessary for all readers.

CHAPTER

1

The Teacher Assessment Movement

It is an exciting time to be an educator. The challenges are greater than they have ever been as one sees society and the world changing with each passing day. Periodically, politicians and the public question the quality of education in America. This questioning often emerges as a reaction to the economy and the increasing need for skilled and knowledgeable workers. As a result numerous national forums, task forces, and commissions are established to study needed reforms. These national committees make recommendations that spawn state task forces, forums, and commissions to initiate the implementation of reform efforts.

The past two decades have seen numerous calls for the reform of public education and significant efforts to respond. The watershed event that brought the perceived shortcomings of education into the forefront of the public consciousness was the publication in 1983 by the National Commission on Excellence in Education of *A Nation at Risk.* The commission's report was on the failings of the nation's educational system and inadvertently led to harsh criticism of the country's teaching force. A decade later, Terrell Bell, who chaired the national commission, stated that the intent of *A Nation at Risk* was to make Americans aware of the needs of its schools and " . . . was not intended for teachers to receive the blame that was heaped on them" (Bell, 1993, p. 593). However, the reality is that the majority of subsequent reform movements has focused on the need to fill our classrooms with competent teachers.

The Carnegie Forum's 1986 study, *A Nation Prepared: Teachers for the 21st Century (Task Force on Teaching as a Profession)*, recognized that 50 years ago American teachers enjoyed the respect they earned as a result of being among the best educated people in the community. Today, teachers are "victims of their own success" (p. 36), for respect for teachers has waned as the education level of the general populace has risen. This "better schooled public" has generated a climate of doubt concerning teachers' competence and their ability to facilitate their students' learning.

The most recent of the national reform efforts is the report of the National Commission on Teaching and America's Future, *What Matters Most: Teaching for America's Future* (1996). Its two-year study concluded that the reform of elementary and secondary education depended primarily on restructuring the teaching profession. The commission's findings reported that, "A caring, competent, and qualified teacher is the most important ingredient in education reform."

Richard Dollase, in his book *Voices of Beginning Teachers: Visions and Realities*, cites a 1989 report of the Association of American Colleges that defines what constitutes a high-quality teacher: " . . . a broadly educated individual who has command of both the subjects to be taught and of the ways which they can be taught effectively to the range of students he or she will be teaching" (p. 1). The quandary is how a nation assures its citizens that this type of teacher resides in all its classrooms with all its children. One way the National Commission suggests is to hold teachers accountable for their teaching and associated duties.

ACCOUNTABILITY

The accountability movement became a part of the educational landscape in the latter part of the twentieth century. Over the past 30 years states have assumed increasing responsibility for schools as the federal government has disbursed education funds to states and, more recently, pushed for deficit reductions. As a result, education has had increased visibility in state budgets and increased attention from legislators. This attention becomes greater as elected state officials explain to their constituencies what kind of education the state money is buying. To provide the public data on how effectively state money is being spent, a push to hold schools accountable for their students' performance has become prevalent (Elmore, 1997).

In the 1970s the teacher empowerment movement began to flow across the nation. Teacher organizations were gaining force to lobby against education budget cutbacks and salary increases lagging behind the cost of living. They supported more involvement of teachers in the development of local curriculum and in the management of local schools. Organizations like the National Education Association (NEA) began to lobby for autonomous professional standards boards that would be involved in program approval processes for teacher education programs, shared governance of these programs, and assessment of classroom teachers. By 1998 fifteen states had established professional standards boards with teachers as the majority of members on each (Berry, 1998).

With growing input and representation in the decision-making process, teachers increasingly are being held accountable for their students' performance. Nearly all states have increased their testing agendas and formulated statewide standards for student performance. Should teachers be held accountable for student learning? Some writers, such as Wang, Haertel, and

Walberg (1990), contend that the extent of student learning in a given year is influenced by many factors that lie beyond the teacher's control. Still many states consider student performance as the center of accountability. It has resulted in mandates for "outcomes assessment" to better measure what students are learning (Kruckeberg, 1995). The pressures of standards and assessments are increasingly present with the classroom teacher being held accountable for student learning.

EVOLUTION OF TEACHER ASSESSMENT

Over the first half of this century, teaching became a profession for women and college-educated minorities who possessed few other options for employment. When young white men did teach, it was usually the first step on their ladder of success to an administrative position or a different profession all together. Since the early 1960s the social demographics have changed. The two-income family has become the rule rather than the exception, and women and minorities have increased opportunities in other fields. These social changes have had a two-fold effect on the number of teachers entering classrooms, particularly in the 1970s. First, the turnover rate for women teachers decreased, which led to fewer job openings for new teacher education graduates. Second, as the opportunities increased in society for women and minorities, these groups prepared for positions with better financial rewards, thus depleting the steady supply of new teachers. When retirements became plentiful beginning in the mid-1980s, emergency and alternative credentialing of non-teacher education majors became prevalent. National reports coupled with the social factors of the last 30 years have been an impetus for teacher assessment (Carnegie Report, 1986).

In the 1970s, competency-based teacher preparation programs emerged. Competencies are knowledge, skills, and behaviors that are stated in advance, can be demonstrated, and are possible to assess. The competency-based movement bore a resemblance to behavioral objectives of the 1960s.

The competency movement also brought major teacher testing initiatives during that decade. These initiatives were tests with multiple-choice questions assessing basic literacy, professional knowledge, and subject matter knowledge (Haertel, 1991). The National Teacher's Exam (NTE) was the most widely used of these tests. These types of tests were later seen to fall short of measuring many important teaching skills and in the 1980s a proliferation of classroom observation instruments was developed to assess teachers' performances. These observation instruments were anchored to teaching effectiveness research, which showed empirical correlations of teaching practices to student achievement. By the early 1980s Florida, Georgia, South Carolina, and North Carolina had performance appraisal instruments in place to assess teaching skills. Many other states soon followed. Though observer evaluations are generally deemed helpful tools, they have inadequacies in assessing some important aspects of teaching (such as, student learning, student assessment, planning, and reflection on teaching.) Additionally, observations by someone else, usually a principal, central office person, or peer, places the responsibility for providing data regarding the teacher's performance into other hands. It is not the teacher, the primary stakeholder who bears the burden of presenting data, but whoever did the observations.

Teaching has always been viewed as a complex set of behaviors and attitudes that converge in the classroom to create the type of interaction conducive to student learning. Teaching is part science and part art, and the research debate on the merits of personal attributes versus technical approaches has raged for several decades (Haertel, 1991). However, most researchers agree that establishing the purpose of evaluation is a critical initial step in the development of a teacher evaluation process or instrument. The observation instruments discussed here had the purpose of assessing if teachers demonstrated a given set of behaviors. The 1986 Carnegie Report helped advance the purpose when it recommended new performance-based assessment instruments using *standards.*

Before progressing into a discussion of new assessment standards, we should clarify how the word *standard* is used. In Edelfelt and Raths's (1998) monograph, *A Brief History of Standards in Teacher Education,* they note that educators have been concerned about standards for more than a century. Pearson (1994) defines standards as ". . . a definite level of degree of quality that is proper or adequate for a specific purpose; something that is established by authority, custom, or general consent as a model or example to be followed." He includes *criterion, gauge, yardstick,* and *test* as alternate words. Today *standard* is used as a synonym for *criterion* (Edelfelt & Raths, p. 3).

In the 1986 Carnegie Report educational reform was charted in the direction of new assessment instruments and standards, with the following suggestions:

- Admission to teacher education programs should be contingent on applicants' mastery of basic skills and knowledge expected of all college graduates.
- States and others should offer incentives for students of exceptional academic ability and to minority candidates who qualify to attend graduate teacher education programs.
- A National Board for Professional Teaching Standards (NBPTS) should be created to establish standards for high levels of professional teaching competencies and to issue certificates to people meeting those standards.
- State and local policy should encourage higher education institutions and other providers to develop programs of continuing education to keep teachers abreast of the field and to prepare them for meeting the NBPTS standards.

The NBPTS proposed by the Carnegie Forum was established in 1987 and has developed (and continues to develop) assessment instruments for the national certification of teachers. The NBPTS assessments provide a rich and complex means of verifying teacher competence using much of the process en-visioned by Lee Shulman, who wrote in 1987:

> I no longer think of assessment of teachers as an activity involving a single test or even a battery of tests. I envision a process that unfolds and extends over time, in which written tests of knowledge, systematic documentation of accomplishments, formal attestations by colleagues and supervisors and analyses of performance in assessment centers and in the workplace are combined and integrated in a variety of ways to achieve a representation of a candidate's pedagogical capacities.

With the impetus of the Carnegie Forum's 1986 statement " . . . [teachers] must demonstrate that they have a command of the needed knowledge and ability to apply it," and Shulman's leadership, the NBPTS assessment emerged. Teachers seeking national certification prepare a portfolio, based upon specific stan-dards, and complete written assessments to measure their content knowledge.

NATIONAL BOARD FOR PROFESSIONAL TEACHING STANDARDS

The NBPTS had begun establishing a "professional model" as opposed to "a bureaucratic model" for teacher assessment. Its process is to determine what knowledge bases and practices teachers must know and be able to do. This professional model is undergirded by the educational beliefs that (1) individ-uals learn more when they are responsible for their own learning and devel-opment and (2) individuals perform at a high level of competence when high expectations and outcomes are clearly stated. This professional model enables teachers to demonstrate and document their competence rather than depend-ing on someone else to document it. The NBPTS standards are listed here and will be discussed in more depth in Chapter 7.

1. Teachers are committed to students and their learning.
2. Teachers know the subjects they teach and how to teach those subjects to students.
3. Teachers are responsible for managing and monitoring student learning.
4. Teachers think systematically about their practice and learn from experience.
5. Teachers are members of a learning community.

The NBPTS standards are designed for experienced, competent teachers who will receive a national certification if they successfully meet the established as-sessment criteria.

The NBPTS process gives experienced teachers the opportunity to take re-sponsibility for demonstrating the depth of their knowledge and skills. To use this professional model with teachers early in their career, new assessment procedures needed to be put in place for them. With new state initiatives, the responsibilities for all teachers are broadening. Beginning and experienced teachers must complete instructional planning for both their classrooms and their schools, participate in the governance of the school, and participate in expanding their knowledge and understanding of students. All these issues pointed to more encompassing means of assessing new teachers' performances. One of the most promising efforts to this end has been the development of assessment standards by the Interstate New Teacher Assessment and Support Consortium (INTASC).

INTASC STANDARDS

INTASC standards were developed under the auspices of the Council of Chief State Officers, a consortium of 37 states dedicated to the basic idea that content knowledge is wedded to pedagogical understanding; if students are to learn, teachers must master these two areas. The INTASC approach requires beginning teachers to demonstrate entry-level competencies of teaching through the development of a portfolio. The INTASC standards possess two important attributes:

1. They are performance-based assessments in which teachers describe what they know and can do once they have entered the profession.
2. They are linked to current views of what students should know and be able to do to meet K-12 standards for learning.

INTASC standards are not rigid in design. They recognize that teachers work in a wide variety of circumstances with populations that are diverse in ethnicity, home language, socioeconomic status, and gender (Ambach, 1996; Shapiro, 1995).

The states and programs that have adopted the INTASC standards have chosen to follow the NBPTS assessment format—the portfolio. Connecticut and North Carolina are two states that have adopted the INTASC standards and have designed licensure procedures using portfolios. The INTASC standards are listed here. These standards are discussed in Chapters 2 and 5.

1. The teacher understands the central concepts, tools of inquiry, and structure of the discipline he or she teaches and can create learning experiences that make these aspects of subject matter meaningful to students.
2. The teacher understands how children learn and develop, and can provide learning opportunities that support a child's intellectual, social, and personal development.

3. The teacher understands how students differ in their approaches to learning and creates instructional opportunities that are adapted to diverse learners.
4. The teacher uses a variety of instructional strategies to encourage student development of critical thinking, problem-solving, and performance skills.
5. The teacher uses an understanding of individual and group motivation and behavior to create a learning environment that encourages social interaction, active engagement in learning, and self-motivation.
6. The teacher uses knowledge of effective verbal, nonverbal, and media communication techniques to foster active inquiry, collaboration, and supportive interaction in the classroom.
7. The teacher plans based upon knowledge of subject matter, students, the community, and curriculum goals.
8. The teacher understands and uses formal and informal assessment strategies to evaluate and ensure the continuous intellectual, social, and physical development of the learner.
9. The teacher is a reflective practitioner who continually evaluates the effects of his or her choices and actions on others (students, parents, and other professionals in the learning community) and who actively seeks out opportunities to grow professionally.
10. The teacher fosters relationships with school colleagues, parents, and agencies in the larger community to support students' learning and well-being.

The NBPTS and INTASC standards are affecting not only the ways teachers are assessed, but also the ways teachers are educated. These standards have been incorporated into the National Council for the Accreditation of Teacher Education (NCATE) accreditation process for teacher preparation programs. New NCATE standards are being developed with increased focus on the performance of the college/university's education graduates.

> The emphasis on performance has been spurred by a realization among policymakers that changes in curriculum and courses have not significantly increased student achievement. The number one factor in enhancing student learning is the capability of the teacher. How to determine quality and knowledge are central questions as NCATE develops its performance-based accreditation system. (Wise, 1998, p. 1)

These new NCATE standards will measure a teacher preparation program by its new graduates' performance—their performance as they move from beginning teachers to continuing teachers. This accountability for colleges and universities is providing the impetus for many to incorporate performance products, such as a portfolio, into their teacher preparation programs. Portfolios for development of preservice teachers are presented in Chapter 4.

CLOSING THOUGHTS

The last decade and a half has spawned numerous national reports on the state of education in America. These reports have generated new assessment instruments using standards that urge educators to be more accountable. The instruments, most prominently used to assess the performance of teachers, have evolved from paper and pencil testing to classroom observations to portfolio development.

Portfolios are a complex assessment process, more so than classroom observation instruments. They provide two distinct advantages over testing and classroom observations. First, portfolios build a professional model of assessment, not a bureaucratic model. They enable teachers to be more "in charge" of their evaluation. Second, though teachers find the portfolios time consuming to compile, they report experiencing considerable professional growth from the process (Hawk, 1996). Because of the professional growth experienced during the development of portfolios, some states reward their teachers for just submitting portfolios to the national board for review. For example, North Carolina awards teachers who submit to NBPTS with 15 continuing education units (the equivalent of 150 clock hours of staff development).

The portfolio type of performance-based product responds to the higher standards as called for in *A Nation Prepared* and *What Matters Most: Teaching for America's Future.* Portfolios enable teachers to (1) demonstrate that they meet the given set of standards, (2) communicate why they are effective and competent, and (3) take charge of their own assessment. They are for preservice, beginning, and experienced teachers. Portfolios have two crucial components: *evidence* that documents teaching and *reflections* that support each piece of evidence. These two components offer teachers at all stages of development the opportunity to grow professionally by collecting and examining teaching materials and, in the process of reflective writing, transform ideas about teaching into clear concepts (Ambach, 1996; Paulson, Paulson, & Meyer, 1991). In Chapter 2, a detailed discussion of portfolios, their purposes, and development will be presented.

REFERENCES

Ambach, G. (1996). Standards for teachers: Potential for improving practice. *Phi Delta Kappan, 78*(3), 207–210.

Bell, T. (1993). Reflections on one decade after *A Nation At Risk. Phi Delta Kappan, 74*(4), 592–597.

Berry, B. (1998). "The growth of professional teacher standards boards." Paper delivered at the National Conference of Professional Teacher Standards Boards, Raleigh, NC, October 1998.

Dollase, R. (1992). *Voices of beginning teachers: Visions and realities.* New York: Teachers College Press.

Edelfelt, R. A. & Raths, J. D. (1998). *A brief history of standards in teacher education.* Washington, DC: Association of Teacher Educators.

Elmore, R. F. (1997). Accountability in local school districts: Learning to do the right things. *Advances in Educational Administration, 5,* 59–82.

Haertel, E. (1991). New forms of teacher assessment. In G. Grant (Ed.), *Review of Research in Education, 17,* 3–30.

Hawk, P. P (1996). *Performance based assessment.* Report to the North Carolina Department of Public Instruction, Raleigh, NC.

Interstate New Teacher Assessment and Support Consortium. (1992). *Model standards for beginning teacher licensing and development: A resource for state dialog.* Washington, DC: Council of Chief State School Officers.

Kruckeberg, D. (1995). *Public relations education and outcomes assessment: An immediate challenge for educators.* Paper presented at the 78th Annual Meeting of the Association for Education in Journalism and Mass Media, Washington, DC, August 1995.

National Commission on Teaching & America's Future (1996). *What matters most: Teaching for America's future.* New York.

Paulson, F., Paulson, P., & Meyer, L. (1991). What makes a portfolio a portfolio? *Educational Leadership, 48*(5), 60–63.

Pearson, P. D. (1994). Standards and teacher education: A policy perception. In M. E. Diez, V. Richardson, & P. Pearson (Eds.), *Setting standards and educating teachers* (pp. 37–67). Washington, DC: American Association of Colleges of Teacher Education.

Shapiro, B. (1995). National standards for teachers. *Streamline Seminars, 13*(4).

Shulman, L. S. (1987). Those who understand: Knowledge growth in teaching. *Educational Researcher, 15*(2), 4–14.

Task Force on Teaching as a Profession (1986). *A nation prepared: Teachers for the 21st century.* New York: Carnegie Forum on Education and the Economy.

Wang, M. C., Haertel, G. D., & Walberg, H. J. (1990). What influences learning? A content analysis of the literature. *Journal of Educational Research, 84,* 30–43.

Wise, A. E. (1998). NCATE 2000 will emphasize candidate performance. *Quality Teaching, 7*(2), 1–2.

C H A P T E R

2

Portfolio Development

WHAT IS A PORTFOLIO?

When people hear the word *portfolio,* many different images come to mind. Artists think of compiling, throughout their career, their best work for review. Along the same lines, a teacher's portfolio often contains gathered samples of lessons, units of study, and professional documents that reflect the knowledge, skills, and beliefs of the teacher. The artist's portfolio describes each painting in writing, giving details about artistic design. The teacher reflects on each piece of work, highlighting strengths, weaknesses, and changes he or she would make in teaching. The teacher's portfolio is used for self-evaluation or external review. Both of these images are correct representations of portfolios, because they both have several specific components:

1. They have a specific **purpose.** The artist's portfolio demonstrates artistic abilities, and the teacher's portfolio shows knowledge, skills, and abilities.
2. They are developed for a specific **audience.** The artist's is a potential employer or buyer, and the teacher's is himself/herself or external reviewers.
3. They contain work samples, commonly called **evidence.** Evidence is the contents put into the portfolio. The artist's evidence would be paintings, pottery, portraits, and/or sculptures. The teacher's evidence would include lesson plans, units of study, and other professional documents.
4. They have **reflections.** Both the artist and teacher would have written thoughts on the evidence contained in the portfolio.

These two examples demonstrate that a product can look different but still be considered a portfolio. A portfolio is not merely a manila file filled with assignments or work, nor is it a scrapbook of memorabilia. Campbell, Cignetti, Melenyzer, Nettles, and Wyman (1997) described a portfolio as an organized, goal-driven collection of evidence. Portfolios have emerged as viable assessment tools for both preservice and inservice teachers. Portfolios are a way for teachers to document their professional development, to measure preservice teacher knowledge, or for purposes of certification (Adams, 1995; Krause, 1996; Tierney, 1993; Wolf, 1996).

There are three different types of portfolios: **process, product,** and **showcase.** While each type is compiled for a different audience, all of them have a developer, a purpose, a specific audience, and a reflection section (discussed in Chapter 3) on the evidence.

A person chooses whether to develop a process, product, or showcase portfolio based on the *purpose* for development. The purpose, which can be described as the "why" of portfolio development, is the driving force that determines the organizational design of the portfolio.

Four Components of Portfolios	Three Types of Portfolios
Purpose	Process
Audience	Product
Evidence	Showcase
Reflections	

WHAT IS A PROCESS PORTFOLIO?

A process portfolio shows a person's performance over a period of time. The purpose of a process portfolio is to evaluate a person's progress in one or more areas over a given period of time. Using writing as an example, the purpose of a process portfolio would be to show how writing is taught in the classroom and how students' writing improved over time. Developers would choose evidence that would show how they taught writing and how their students progressed over time. Reflections would focus on how writing was taught and how students developed writing skills and abilities.

For example, a teacher might describe a lesson focusing on writing and identify successes and areas in which students need to improve at this point. Then, the teacher would reflect on what should happen next in the classroom in relation to writing. Evidence would be chosen as the portfolio is developed over the school year. Evidence would represent successes and weaknesses of the writing program so a clear portrayal of the teacher's progress is given. Different teachers using writing as a focus could have different evidence, depending on their own development. The process portfolio is commonly used by teachers who want to focus on the development of skills and knowledge.

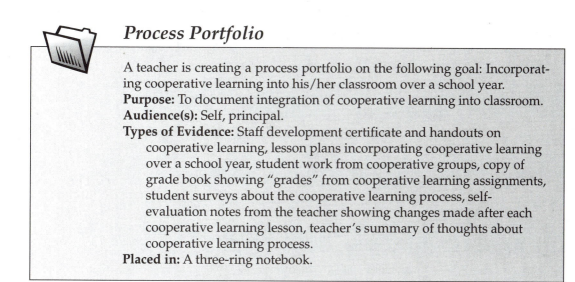

Process Portfolio

A teacher is creating a process portfolio on the following goal: Incorporating cooperative learning into his/her classroom over a school year.
Purpose: To document integration of cooperative learning into classroom.
Audience(s): Self, principal.
Types of Evidence: Staff development certificate and handouts on cooperative learning, lesson plans incorporating cooperative learning over a school year, student work from cooperative groups, copy of grade book showing "grades" from cooperative learning assignments, student surveys about the cooperative learning process, self-evaluation notes from the teacher showing changes made after each cooperative learning lesson, teacher's summary of thoughts about cooperative learning process.
Placed in: A three-ring notebook.

The First Portfolio!

"I kept saying, 'Maybe we should clean off the front of the refrigerator' —but, nooo . . ."

Cartoon by Art Bouthillier. All rights reserved.

Sample Process Portfolio

Background: Mr. Clark, a kindergarten grade teacher is interested in developing a portfolio to show his progress as a teacher, specifically in using developmentally appropriate practices. He wants to show his knowledge, skills, and abilities in this area.

Purpose: To track progress as a teacher using developmentally appropriate practices.

Audience: Mr. Clark and principal.

Developer: Mr. Clark.

Organization: Portfolio is kept in a three-ring notebook.

Evidence: Mr. Clark chooses evidence throughout the year related to using developmentally appropriate practices (DAP). He included the following evidence:

1. A philosophical statement about the use of DAP in the classroom
2. Lesson plans documenting the use of DAP (several subjects over year)
3. Unit plans documenting use of DAP (several over year)
4. Videotape showing several lessons—one in September, one in December, one in March, and one in May
5. Journal by teacher documenting on a day-to-day basis the implementation of DAP
6. Student work from several different students (at different levels) throughout the year
7. Anecdotal records documenting progress of students throughout year
8. Entries in teacher's journal comparing DAP strategies with those previously used

Other evidence would be determined by Mr. Clark depending on the progress of his portfolio.

Reflections: Mr. Clark writes reflections about his progress each month. At the end of the year, he writes a summary and an analysis of the entire process.

Assessment: Mr. Clark does a self-assessment through writing reflections each month, and his principal assesses his progress at the end of the school year. Based on Mr. Clark's self-assessments and the principal's summative assessment, Mr. Clark determines his next steps in relation to using DAP.

Why is a process portfolio chosen? Mr. Clark wants to track his progress over a year. Each teacher may have a different timeline for his/her progress.

WHAT IS A PRODUCT PORTFOLIO?

A product portfolio is a specific set of evidence developed over a short period of time to meet a desired outcome. This type of portfolio is similar to a project. Each person developing a product portfolio has identical or very similar pieces of evidence. For teachers, product portfolios would be created around a particular goal or initiative. Teachers may create them to show how a school goal is being met, to seek a license, or to compete for an award. Any time teachers need to be compared using the same criteria, a product portfolio is a valid measure. This portfolio has specific, required evidence so assessors can compare developers consistently against the set criteria.

Product Portfolio

Each teacher is creating a portfolio to show the implementation of a school-wide discipline program.

Purpose: To document how each teacher participates in and supports the new schoolwide discipline approach.

Audience: Teacher, principal.

Types of Evidence: Listing of rules and procedures, copy of discipline log for each class (part of plan), parent contact log, parent conference record, motivation incentives.

Placed in: An expandable folder.

Using writing again, a teacher's product portfolio could be developed to show the implementation of the "writing process" (steps including brainstorming, draft writings, editing, revising, and final draft of the written product) in the classroom. Imagine that a district sets a goal that each teacher will use the writing process in his/her classroom, regardless of subject(s) taught. The purpose would be to show how a teacher implements the writing process into day-to-day classroom activities, lesson plans, unit plans, and student assessment methods. For example, each portfolio could contain staff development information, lesson plans, unit plans, student work demonstrating each step of the writing process, and assessment rubrics or checklists. Reflections would include descriptions of how the writing process was included in the classroom, what are the strengths and areas in need of improvement for implementing the writing process, and how changes would be made during the next lesson or unit. All portfolios developed would all be assessed using the same criteria, probably by the principal in this example.

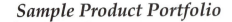

Sample Product Portfolio

Background: Jane Goodman, a middle level educator, teaches science to
students in the seventh grade. As part of a district initiative, all science
teachers are implementing a lab-based curriculum. The prescriptive
curriculum has a teacher's manual with lab procedures for the entire
school year (one concept per week/28 weeks).

Purpose: To document the implementation of the lab-based science
curriculum across the district.

Audience: District science supervisor.

Organization: Notebook is divided into 28 sections.

Evidence: Student work samples and lesson plans are included for each of
the 28 sections.

Reflection: Ms. Goodman writes a reflection at the end of each week and
at the end of the school year.

Assessment: The district supervisor reviews the portfolio. In addition, the
supervisor interviews the teacher individually and holds small group
conferences with clusters of teachers. The portfolio is used as the basis
for these assessment activities. The results of these conferences,
interviews, and portfolio contents allow the district supervisor and
teacher to set goals for the next year.

Why is a product portfolio chosen? The district supervisor chooses a
product portfolio because she wants to compare how teachers
implement the new curriculum. By choosing a product portfolio, she
can see the strengths and weaknesses of the curriculum as a whole
and in use by individuals teachers.

WHAT IS A SHOWCASE PORTFOLIO?

Showcase portfolios are collections of a person's best work chosen by the individual. These portfolios are often used for job interviews or teacher-of-the-year
competitions. The purpose of the portfolio is for teachers to showcase their
best work in one or more areas.

Showcase Portfolio

A high school math teacher is searching for a job. He creates a showcase
portfolio.

Purpose: To gain employment in teaching.

Audience: Potential employers.

Showcase Portfolio—continued

Types of Evidence: Sample lesson plans, classroom management plans, teaching evaluations, college transcripts, letters from students and student teaching supervisors, philosophy of education paper, resume, pictures of students taught, videotape of teaching, sample student work.
Placed in: Three-ring binder.

For example, the teacher could develop a showcase portfolio to prepare for a teaching award. The portfolio would contain evidence chosen by the developer. This evidence would be what the developer believes to be his/her best work in teaching. Some developers might place several best lessons in their showcase portfolio while other teachers might add a series of lessons that highlight various teaching strategies. Reflections for any showcase portfolio would focus on why evidence was chosen and why it is deemed as "best work." The main idea of this portfolio is that the developer chooses what to showcase and how to organize it. Unlike the other two types, this portfolio is completely individualized and is based on the developer's perceptions about himself or herself.

Sample Showcase Portfolio

Background: Mark Smith is a business education teacher looking for a high school teaching position.
Purpose: To obtain teaching position.
Developer: Mr. Smith.
Organization: The evidence is collected in a three-ring binder under four areas determined by Mr. Smith: *teaching, management, computer skills* and *knowledge* (since this would be an integral part of the business curriculum), and *involving parents and the community*.
Evidence: Mr. Smith includes sample evidence under each area. Sample evidence includes: lesson plans, unit plans, student work, videotapes and pictures of teaching, resume, philosophy of education position paper, management plan, classroom rules, sample work using different computer software (including processed documents showing word processing skills and spreadsheets), samples of letters sent to parents, and a parent communication plan.
Reflection: A reflection is written for each area. He answers the following questions: (1) Why was the evidence chosen? (2) What are the strengths of the work?
Assessment: The person who interviews Mr. Smith.

WHAT ARE THE DIFFERENCES IN THE THREE PORTFOLIOS?

All three types of portfolios are purposeful collections of evidence with thoughtful reflections. The difference between the three types of portfolios involves three components: (1) the purpose of the portfolio, (2) what type of evidence is collected, and (3) how the evidence is collected. The what and how of evidence collection is a direct result of the portfolio's purpose. For example, in a process portfolio with a purpose of showing progress of teaching skills, the what of evidence would be a collection of documents that show the obtainment of teaching skills and the how would be the developer's choice. For the product portfolio with the purpose of demonstrating the use of a specific teaching strategy, the how and what are the same for all developers. In a showcase portfolio with the purpose of highlighting a teacher's best teaching skills, the how and what of evidence are both determined by the developer. Table 2–1 compares how the different types of portfolios might be used to assess a school goal.

Check for Understanding

It is important for readers of this book to develop an understanding of content prior to moving to the next section. Use the following questions to check comprehension.

1. What are the three types of portfolios?
2. What are the differences between the three types?
3. What are the four common components of all portfolios?
4. Give an example for each type of portfolio.

If all questions were answered correctly, you are ready to move on to the next section. If all answers were not clear, reread part or all of this section.

WHAT IS A TEACHING PORTFOLIO?

Portfolios, in general, are used by professionals in many different types of careers. A teaching portfolio is specific to the education profession. Shulman (1994) defines a teaching portfolio as "a carefully selected set of coached or mentored accomplishments substantiated by samples of student work and fully realized only through reflective writing, deliberation, and serious conversation. (p. 8)"

TABLE 2–1   *Different Types of Portfolios for Elementary Teachers*

Background: An elementary school has implemented a new reading program. The principal has decided to require teachers to build portfolios in relation to the reading program. This chart shows how each type of portfolio can be used in relation to the new reading program. The teachers are the **developers.** All three types of portfolios, process, product, and showcase, are identified with the four components outlined for each.

Type	Purpose	Audience	Sample Evidence	Reflection Focus
Process	To show teacher's individual growth in using the new reading program over one year	Principal, Teacher*	1. Lesson plans showing reading program being implemented 2. Student work 3. Audiotapes of various students' reading once a month for the school year 4. Running records showing successful and struggling students' progress over the year 5. Parent conference write-ups indicating the new program had been implemented	For each piece of evidence, the teacher could describe how it is related to the reading program and the strengths and weaknesses of implementing the program.
Product	To show each teacher had implemented specific components of the reading program	Principal	Specific components outlined by the principal at the beginning of the year. Each teacher would have the same types of evidence, for example, all teachers might be required to have lesson plans showing the correlation to the reading program.	The teacher would focus on the strengths of the required evidence.
Showcase	For teachers to show their best work in relation to implementing the reading program	Principal	Teachers would choose evidence that shows their best attempts at implementing the reading program. This could include: 1. effective lesson plans 2. excellent student work 3. running records of students who showed great progress	The teacher would reflect on each piece of evidence, emphasizing the strengths of the evidence in relation to the reading program.

*For improving teaching

Teachers can develop portfolios at any stage of their career. This can begin with preservice teachers at the university level who are preparing to enter the profession and progress to those who are master teachers who choose to apply for national board certification. A teaching portfolio contains evidence that shows the knowledge, skills, abilities, and dispositions of teachers at their particular stage of development. The portfolio is usually organized around the central components of teaching, including planning and teaching curriculum, student-centered instruction, student development, strategies, assessment practices, classroom management procedures, and professional development opportunities. Evidence in a teacher's portfolio would minimally include lesson plans, classroom procedures and management plan, sample tests, student work, professional conference materials, committee work, and parent contact logs. For each of these entries, a written reflection would be included.

A teacher's portfolio is a useful component for a teacher at any stage of development. Preservice teachers are acquiring the skills and knowledge to teach from their college or university program. Through a portfolio, they can document their acquisition of knowledge about teaching and their ability to teach. University faculty can have preservice teachers reflect upon their emerging abilities and knowledge. Over the 2 to 3 years preservice teachers are in their teaching programs, their views and concrete knowledge about teaching change quickly. Evidence and reflections can help document their rapidly changing views and knowledge.

Once preservice teachers complete the required components of their teacher education program, they enter the induction phase of their career. The induction phase encompasses the first to fourth years of a teacher's career. During this induction period, the teacher is commonly called a beginning teacher. At the onset of this stage, most beginning teachers have a probationary license, which allows them to teach during this trial period of 1 to 4 years.

Teaching portfolios in the initial phase are used for licensure purposes and/or reemployment. In this portfolio, beginning teachers create portfolios that document their ability to teach effectively.

At the end of their probationary period (length determined by each state), beginning teachers move from holding an initial license to a continuing license (one that is renewable with course or workshop credit every 5 years or so). At this time, teachers usually have tenure. As a continuing teacher, the teaching portfolio becomes an option to demonstrate professional growth. This type of growth is based on personal needs and/or interests. For example, a teacher might be interested in learning more about children's learning styles (Dunn & Dunn, 1978) and implementing this theoretical approach in his/her classroom. In the teaching portfolio, evidence would include information received about learning styles and samples of implementing this approach in the classroom. Evidence could include the new classroom layout showing learning styles centers, lesson plans emphasizing the approach, and classroom procedures that support the change. Portfolios for professional development are an option to traditional evaluation methods for teachers, such as principal observations.

Continuing teachers have tenure so the portfolio option frequently becomes their choice. However, in some states portfolios are used as an assessment tool for teacher licensure renewal. These renewal cycles are usually 5 years in length.

Once teachers have taught for 5 years or more, they usually enter the next stage of their career, the master teacher stage. The master teacher is one who would have the skills, knowledge, and beliefs reflective in the national board standards. These teachers can choose to apply for national board certification through the NBPTS. Successful teaching portfolios compiled for national board certification demonstrate how teachers are at the top of their field against a set of standards. The teaching portfolio at this stage is an option for teachers.

No matter what stage a teacher is in, a teaching portfolio can be developed. The purpose of the portfolio changes at each stage of a teacher's career. However, at each stage the portfolio would contain evidence related to teaching and reflections that outline the teacher's knowledge, abilities, and beliefs. Figure 2–1 lists examples of portfolio evidence. Refer to different chapters in this book for information and examples of teaching portfolios at different levels.

• **Lesson plans**	• **Classroom rules**
• **Unit plans**	• **Parent communication**
• **Philosophy of education paper**	• **Team newsletters**
• **Pictures of classroom activities**	• **Professional development certificates**
• **Videotapes of lessons taught**	• **State curriculum correlation with lesson**
• **Student work**	**plan**
• **Differentiation methods for exceptional**	• **Pacing guides**
children	• **Test preparation strategies**
• **Case studies**	• **Listing of motivation strategies**
• **Action research projects**	• **Grading policies**
• **Lesson plans showing varied teaching and**	• **Department or grade level meeting minutes**
learning strategies	• **Committee memberships**
• **Planning guides**	• **School newsletters with highlights of class**
• **Copies of lesson plan book**	**accomplishments**
• **Community involvement**	• **Field trip information (with students)**
• **Photos of student performances**	• **Classroom floor plans**
• **Letters from students and parents**	• **Technology competencies of teacher**
• **Photos of student work**	• **Peer reviews**
• **Workshops attended (certificates)**	• **Self-evaluations**
• **Position papers**	• **Professional development plans**
• **Student projects**	• **Transcripts**
• **Parent volunteer information**	• **Volunteer work (teacher)**
• **Classroom organization strategies**	• **Related work experience**
• **Teacher projects**	

Compiled by the authors from a review of more than 300 portfolios

FIGURE 2–1   Types of Portfolio Evidence

Check for Understanding

1. What is a teaching portfolio?
2. How is a teaching portfolio different from other professionals' (such as artists') portfolios?

LEGAL ISSUES IN PORTFOLIO DEVELOPMENT

No teacher can create or design a teaching portfolio without reviewing the legal parameters. Teachers, in particular, are sensitive to children's rights and want to portray an image of doing the right thing in relation to the privacy issues of their students. The rule of thumb for legal issues is to consider the audience. If the audience is someone in addition to or other than the developer, immediate supervisor (i.e., principal), or state licensing agency, students' parents should sign a release form allowing their children's work to be included in the portfolio. Many school districts have release forms on file. Teachers should also send an informational letter explaining the purpose of the portfolio. These two items can be combined, as demonstrated in the sample letter in Figure 2–2. If the developer is submitting the portfolio to an immediate supervisor or to a licensing agency, no release forms are needed.

While the release form is the mainstay in legal defensibility, the following guidelines are good to follow to uphold the ethical rights of teachers, especially if the audience is external:

1. Mark out all students' names.
2. Refer to students anonymously in reflections.
3. Don't identify students in pictures.
4. Be sensitive about exceptional children. Don't include them by name or by picture in a portfolio.

The best advice is, first, to check school policies regarding legal issues and, second, to use common sense when deciding about types of evidence. The legal issues related to portfolios are not extensive, but guidelines involving ethics and courtesy should be followed.

Videotaping is another area of consideration in terms of legal requirements. Many districts require a release for videotaping. Teachers should keep these releases on file. Those students whose parents would not give permission should not be included in the videotape. Federal law specifies that children with special needs should not be videotaped.

Check for Understanding

1. When must you use a release form?
2. What are ethical guidelines to follow when building a portfolio?

Sept. 1, 2000

Dear Parents,

I am a student teacher in Mrs. Adams's class at Bright Days Elementary School. As part of my college requirements, I am creating a teaching portfolio. I would like to include sample work of your child. Your child's name will not appear on any work included or in the written text describing it. Your signature below allows me to include your child's work in my portfolio. Thank you for your support. Feel free to contact Mrs. Adams if you have any questions.

Sincerely,

Ms. Lee

I give permission for my child's work to be included in Ms. Lee's teaching portfolio.

Parent's Signature _____

Date _____

FIGURE 2–2   Sample Personalized Release Form

GENERAL CONSIDERATIONS FOR DEVELOPING PORTFOLIOS

After teachers decide on the purpose of their portfolio, they should follow these general guidelines, regardless of their stage of development. Further information for specific teacher stages is described in later chapters. General guidelines include:

1. **Save everything.** Either throw samples in a box in the classroom or create files for different types of evidence.
2. **Choose a container.** Portfolios can be placed in three-ring binders, file boxes, or folders. Binders are the most common types of containers used by developers.
3. **For external reviews, use plastic sheets to house evidence.** This will give the portfolio a professional look and keep evidence neat.
4. **Create a professional cover.** This will give reviewers a positive first impression. The developer's name and picture are minimal components. Inspiring quotes, clip art, borders, and a title add character to the cover page.

5. **Organize the portfolio.** If the portfolio is developed for external audiences, a table of contents is key. Tabbing different sections allows for easy access. These small features allow reviewers to view the contents easily.
6. **Begin with an introductory section.** Developers should include a section on themselves that includes a resume and other pertinent information, such as letters of reference and a philosophical statement.
7. **Word-process everything.** Cover sheets, sections, table of contents, tabs, etc., should not be handwritten. A professional appearance is crucial.
8. **Doublecheck spelling and grammar.** Developers should use standard English and proofread their work. Enlist help from a colleague if needed. Again, professional work is important.
9. **Add voice narration to videotapes.** If a videotape is chosen or required as evidence, developers should make sure their voice is heard when taping. While the videotape does not have to be professional, reviewers want to hear the teacher's voice. Enlist a colleague to help with videotaping.
10. **Hone your videotaping skills.** Use a tripod, check for glare, have light in the background, do a sound check, and alleviate extraneous sounds. Consider a practice run to check for these components.
11. **Focus on videotape content.** Watch your videotape to ensure that its purpose has been achieved. Watching the tape from a teaching and learning perspective will allow you to "see" the taped episode from both the teacher's and students' views.

CLOSING THOUGHTS

This chapter has given readers an overview of types and general logistics of portfolio development. The portfolio is a powerful assessment tool for teachers. Its ability to "tell the story" of the developer allows for depth and breadth that isn't possible through any other medium. Specific portfolio types allow teachers to choose evidence demonstrating a defined purpose, resulting in an effective product.

REFERENCES

Adams, T. L. (1995). A paradigm for portfolio assessment in teacher education. *Education, 115,* 658–570, 528.

Campbell, D. M., Cignetti, P. B., Melenyzer, B. J., Nettles, D. H, & Wyman, R. M. Jr. (1997). *How to develop a professional portfolio.* Boston: Allyn and Bacon.

Dunn, R., & Dunn, K. (1978). *Teaching students through their individual learning styles: A practical approach.* Englewood Cliffs, NJ: Prentice Hall.

Krause, S. (1996). Portfolios in teacher education: Effects of instruction on preservice teachers' early comprehension of the portfolio process. *Journal of Teacher Education, 47,* 130–138.

Shulman, L. S. (1994, January). *Portfolios in historical perspective.* Presentation at the Portfolios in Teaching and Teacher Education Conference, Cambridge, MA.

Tierney, D. S. (1993). *Teaching portfolios: 1992 update on research and practice.* Berkeley, CA: Far West Laboratory for Educational Research and Development.

Wolf, K. (1996). Developing an effective teaching portfolio. *Educational Leadership, 53*(6), 34–37.

3

Reflection

Reflection is a key component in portfolio development. It requires developers to think about what they are doing, why they are doing it, what the outcomes are, and how the information can be used for continuous improvement (McLaughlin & Vogt, 1998). Without a written reflection, a portfolio becomes a scrapbook. Reflections tell readers what developers value about their teaching. The written words that comprise reflections allow readers to hear developers' voices in relation to evidence included in the portfolios. Essentially, the reflection is the "glue" of the portfolio: it gives substance to the collection and guides readers. Reflection allows individuals to improve and grow. The role of reflection in portfolio assessment complements the idea of the teacher as a reflective practitioner. Reflection is a significant component of the portfolio process for professionals.

The emphasis on teacher reflection grows out of a body of literature that emerged during the 1980s, which describes the need for, approaches to, and benefits from reflection (Cady, 1998, Sparks-Langer & Colton, 1991). As educators engage in instruction and then reflect on it, the process offers insights into various dimensions of teaching and learning that can lead to better teaching (Schon, 1987). If professionals never reflect on their actions or beliefs, they miss valuable opportunities to improve their teaching.

WHAT IS REFLECTION?

Reflection is the process of assessing information or events, thinking about and analyzing them, and then using the results to change or enhance future events. In education, teachers reflect consistently on their own practice and on the achievement of their students. Teaching reflections consist of three vital components: (1) description, (2) analysis, and (3) planning (see Figure 3–1).

To begin the process of reflection, a *description* is important. The description should emphasize the following: who, what, when, where, and how. The

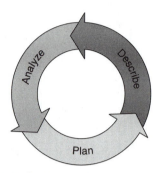

FIGURE 3–1 The Teacher's Reflection Cycle

Three Stages of Reflection	
1. description	3. planning
2. analysis	

description component provides the foundation for the rest of the reflection. This is an important segment for the audience of the portfolio—and for the developer. If a clear description is provided, the other two components of the reflection will be easier to write.

Reflection One: Sample Description by Preservice Teacher

This piece of evidence is a math lesson on "volume of prisms, cylinders, pyramids, and cones" taught to a seventh grade class with a diverse population of students with varied learning abilities. Things considered when planning this lesson were (1) the prior knowledge of the students, and (2) the fact this class has children who become disengaged easily. As a result of these factors, I filled my lesson with various activities that required participation. During my planning, I developed pictures and models for students so they would understand the concept I was teaching.

When teaching this lesson, I took on the role of a coach. I gave instruction and then allowed students time to do activities. I informally assessed students during the activities. I looked at students' body language, facial expression, interest, effort, and ability to get the "right" answer. If they seemed to have an interest, positive body language, and an ability to get the "right"

Reflection One: Sample Description by Preservice Teacher—continued

answer, I would move on in the lesson. However, if they failed to possess these things, I would reteach, review, and/or give another example for them to work. This choice was based on what signals I received from the students.

This math lesson addressed the state math curriculum goal, "demonstrate an understanding and use of measurement." I did this by instructing students how to use the measurement of volume with geometric figures like cylinders, prisms, and cones. In the lesson, I used both pictures and models to allow students to have a representation of the abstract concept of volume. This helped students who were visual and kinesthetic to receive instruction in a form they could easily understand.

Next, the developer *analyzes* the evidence. Analysis means to break the whole apart and analyze it for patterns. Patterns can be analyzed in terms of strengths and areas to improve. In this stage, the developer identifies strengths of the evidence and areas on which to improve. For example, if a lesson plan were included, the developer would outline the positive components of the plan and its implementation and then emphasize areas to improve the next lesson. Teachers who write thoughtful reflections are honest about their own strengths and weaknesses. Some evidence, such as a workshop certificate, may not require developers to reflect on how they might improve. The developers must determine if the certificate is relevant as a piece of evidence.

Reflection One: Sample Analysis by a Preservice Teacher

The lesson's successfulness can be addressed from two perspectives. One, the lesson was successful because students participated, and through informal assessment, students seemed to be understanding the content addressed within the lesson. Two, the lesson was not successful because it did not cover all the content and I insisted on perfection. The content was not covered in a very efficient or effective manner. I seemed to dwell on drilling the students on concepts they already understood, which took away from quality instruction time. I also insisted on perfection from students on each aspect of the lesson before I was willing to move on to the next aspect to be covered. Therefore, I ran out of time before all content was addressed.

The final stage of reflection, *planning,* is perhaps the most important. In this stage, the developers write about how the evidence has influenced them and the implications for their future teaching based on this evidence.

Reflection One: Planning by a Preservice Teacher

Teaching this lesson taught me that assessment was necessary and drilling was not necessary. I need to set my goals at an achievable level for students. Through this teaching experience I saw firsthand how assessment was essential in good teaching. It is essential because it allows instruction to be centered around what students know and what they need to know. I learned that assessing students within a lesson can help pinpoint the instruction method that works best with the content, environment, and students. Second, I found that drilling was not necessary. I discovered that it is boring for students. Drilling is boring because students are not challenged to think for themselves but to simply repeat back what others have already thought through. In the future, I plan to assess students informally in a way that would allow them to think through, for themselves, the content I am teaching. Third, I want to set an achievable level for students. In this lesson, I almost set my students up for failure because the achievement level I had for them was mastery. I realized that very few people will become "masters" of a content area. Therefore, I should not set my students up for mastery, but rather for an achievable goal. In this lesson, I should have emphasized their ability to think through a problem as my achievable goal for the lesson. Instead, I resorted to a mastery level for students. The level I chose was that the students had to answer each informal assessment topic correctly before being able to move on to any other content instruction. I do not think that extremes are essential; however, I do believe it is necessary for students to have a good understanding of a content area before moving on to related content areas. I think this is necessary so that poper background understanding of the content area can be formed by the student. This content understanding will allow new content understanding to be established more easily in a student's mind.

Overall, I was extremely pleased with the lesson plan, the teaching experience, and the outcomes that the lesson brought in both the students' content understandings and in my own professional understanding.

After reading the three sections of this reflection, let's consider a few attributes.

1. It is written in first person. This is appropriate for any reflection written for a portfolio, because the reflection is a personal account of the evidence and reactions to it.

2. The reflection is an accurate description and goes beyond superficial analysis.
3. It is well written. The reflection is clear and free of grammatical and spelling errors.Writing well is a difficult task. Making an effort to write clearly and concisely adds quality to the portfolio.
4. The content is accurate and honest. Reflections should provide an accurate description and analysis of the evidence. This sample reflection shows the teacher's ability to write about her strengths and weaknesses in connection to teaching the lesson plan. This provides insight into her development as a professional. If the reflection were superficial, it would be less informative and effective.

WHY SHOULD TEACHERS REFLECT?

Reflection is deemed an important component of the teaching profession. INTASC, NBPTS, and Pathwise (PRAXIS III) formalize the expectations for teaching reflection (Cady, 1998). One of the five tenets of national board certification is the ability to reflect on practice. The tenet states, "Teachers think systematically about their practice and learn from experience." Board-certified teachers are models of educated persons who strive to strengthen their teaching. These nationally certified teachers critically examine their practice and use this information to change and/or enhance their practices (NBPTS, 1996). In addition, most preservice teacher education programs incorporate reflection into each class. At this stage, preservice teachers use reflection to develop skills, knowledge, and abilities. Inservice teachers use reflection to refine teaching skills and during evaluation sessions with principals and supervisors. These examples show how reflection is seen as a vital component of each stage of teacher development. As teachers engage in reflection, they become more thoughtful about their practice and, consequently, more effective teachers.

Check for Understanding

1. What are the three components of reflection?
2. Why is reflection important for teachers?
3. What role does reflection play in portfolio development?

CHECKLIST FOR REFLECTION WRITERS

Developers should consider four areas as they write their reflections: audience, clear writing, voice, and bias. These areas should also be used as a checklist as the reflections are edited.

Audience   When writing, first consider your audience. As you write, keep your audience in mind at all times. If the audience is a potential employer, the reflection should be written with principals or other supervisors in mind. Knowing your audience allows you to write purposefully.

Clear Writing   A reflection that is well written enhances any portfolio. Pay specific attention to grammar and spelling. It is especially important for teachers to write clearly since this is expected as a basic skill. When writing reflections, record thoughts first and then edit. Appropriate professional language should be used for all reflections.

Voice   Make sure your voice is clearly evident in the tone and content of your reflection. This is a personal reflection, so writing in first person is appropriate. Use "I" and "me" instead of the less personal "the author." Make it clear to your audience that you are expressing your thoughts.

Bias   Be sensitive to ethnicity, gender, and children with special needs when writing a reflection. Use currently accepted terms for all ethnic groups and sensitive language when discussing students with special educational needs. To present yourself as a professional, take care not to offend any audience member who would read the portfolio.

Bias is often a difficult topic for people to discuss openly. When reading other people's writing, preconceptions and stereotypes about diversity can interfere. For example, a teacher might list the demographics of the classroom: "The class had 14 Caucasian students and 13 African-American students." The listing of ethnic percentages might seem commonplace in today's schools to many readers but some might consider the reference to ethnicity as biased because it labels certain groups of children. It is helpful to have someone else read reflections to review for bias and question the inclusion of potentially sensitive material.

REFLECTION ACTIVITIES TO GET YOU STARTED

One way to write good reflections is to begin by studying models of good and bad reflections and analyzing them in terms of strengths and weaknesses. Read each of the following reflections and analyze them in terms of (1) the stages of reflection, and (2) the four areas of consideration (audience, clear writing, voice, and bias).

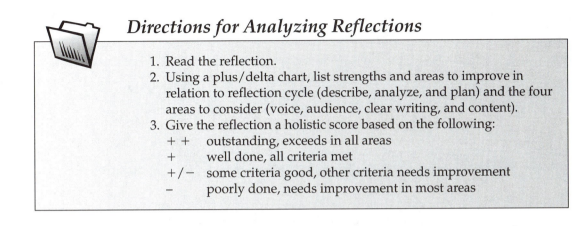

Directions for Analyzing Reflections

1. Read the reflection.
2. Using a plus/delta chart, list strengths and areas to improve in relation to reflection cycle (describe, analyze, and plan) and the four areas to consider (voice, audience, clear writing, and content).
3. Give the reflection a holistic score based on the following:

   + +   outstanding, exceeds in all areas
   +   well done, all criteria met
   + / − some criteria good, other criteria needs improvement
   −   poorly done, needs improvement in most areas

For the first scoring opportunity, reread the reflection presented in three parts earlier in this chapter and consider how you would score it using the holistic scoring guide (+ +, +, +/−, −). See Appendix A for the author's response to this reflection.

Now read the following two reflections on a science lesson and a videotaped lesson, and follow the same directions to analyze and score them.

Reflection Two: A Science Lesson

Description: I taught a science lesson to a group of seventh grade boys and girls from diverse ethnic backgrounds. Most of the students in this class are struggling and several are repeating this grade for the second year. Many of the students are challenging, in terms of behavior. The lesson focused on simple machines. I began by having the students write a few notes about what they knew about simple machines. Then we brainstormed together about things we see every day that might be simple machines. Everyone was involved in the discussion. Next I spent 15 to 20 minutes describing each of the six simple machines and demonstrating with models. The students were able to watch, to reflect, and then to work with the simple machines. We discussed as a large group, worked in small groups that I supervised, and reflected individually about what we wrote, what we saw, and what we touched. In addition, I encouraged vocabulary building and note taking with a handout we completed together. During the time left at the end of class, the students worked on hidden word puzzles I created just for this lesson.

Since I have taught this class for several weeks, I was very aware of the importance of keeping the students involved, of keeping the lesson going, and of constantly reinforcing the information in a variety of ways (discussion, hands-on, note taking, games). I wanted the information to be accessible. I

Reflection Two: A Science Lesson—continued

gave illustrations of simple machines using things the students are familiar with. I was pleased when one child made the connection between an inclined plane and ramps for wheelchairs at the hospital where his mother works, and when another made the connection between a pulley and an elevator. All the students were interested in handling the simple machines I brought in during the lesson. Some of the definitions and equations took more time than I anticipated, so I had to skip the "independent practice" section of my lesson plan, but I thought it was important to teach how simple machines are a part of our everyday lives.

Analysis: I used the textbook as the lesson's foundation, but I constructed my own teaching props, and there was a good deal of interest because of the immediacy of the subject material. The lesson was very successful. My students were even able to reduce some complicated machines in the world around them to simple terms. Science helped them to explain the world. I showed them that science is useful and that it is valuable because it is useful. The least effective part of the lesson was the puzzle, because it was not clear enough to be useful as a reinforcement tool. I had to do more explaining than I wanted to. Overall, the class was not quiet during the lesson, but much of the noise was constructive. For the most part, my students all stayed on task. The lesson probably included a little more information than could be efficiently mastered in one lesson. The introduction of the simple machines alone, without definitions and equations, would have been more than enough; but, all in all, the lesson was a positive experience for myself and for my students.

Planning: This lesson showed me the value of making academic information relevant and real (see, feel, touch, hold). This class is very social and active, and this type of lesson lent itself to group interaction and discussion. I was able to use these strategies effectively because I was prepared. Maintaining control of the classroom is easier when students are interested, and it is up to me as a teacher to help them see why they should be interested. It is necessary to acknowledge where they are (their need for social interaction) and to recognize what tools will most efficiently get them to where I want them to be. This lesson reinforced the importance of preparation and appropriate teaching strategies based on the needs of my students and the information I am teaching.

Reflection Three: A Videotaped Lesson

Description: This piece of evidence is a videotape of a lesson I taught to a general math class. The lesson was on two- and three-digit divisions in which I reviewed students for the standardized test. The videotape was a requirement for a class, but I am glad it was. It was required to allow me to evaluate myself teaching and to determine how effective the lesson was. The lesson was taught using an overhead projector and the students also worked out problems on the chalkboard. The strategy used for teaching the lesson was mini-lecture. The [clinical] teacher wanted me to teach the lesson this particular way.

The videotape of the lesson is related to teaching because a teacher should constantly evaluate himself or herself to see how effective the lesson was and what if any changes that can be made. A teacher should be a reflective practitioner who continually assesses the effects of his or her choices and action on others; this helps the teacher grow professionally. The teacher should also use the videotape to teach the same lesson at a later date.

Analysis: I believe the lesson went all right but it could have gone better. Some students participated, while others didn't. The students were alert mostly because they know that the lesson was being videotaped. They also knew that their teacher was watching them [clinical teacher]. While I was teaching, I felt as if the lesson was somewhat effective. But after watching the videotape, I felt differently. The students were bored with the lesson. Some were yawning and others had their head down.

One strength of the lesson was that the students seems as if they know the material I was teaching or the lesson was a review for the standardized test. The ones that did participate knew all the answers and could work the problems independently. There were several weaknesses of the lesson. One weakness was that I wasn't aware of the things that were going on around me. When viewing the video, I saw students talking, yawning, and even passing notes. Evidently, the students did all of these things while I was working our problems on the overhead. This really irritated me.

Planning: In future lessons, I need to be more creative with my lessons. The plans should be more student-oriented. I know from this experience that overhead projectors will be of minimal use in my classroom and when I use them, the students will teach the lesson using the projector. When I start teaching, I don't think that I will lecture a lot to my students either.

As a teacher, I have to be aware of my classroom environment. Students will take advantage of you, if you let them and they will also do things behind your back. I have to move around my classroom to make sure the students are on task. This videotape really helped me out and I'm glad that we were required to do it.

TAKING THE NEXT STEP

The process of reflecting becomes easier the more one does it. If this process seems overwhelming, try going through the following steps to help develop reflection skills for each of the three stages: description, analysis, and future impact.

Description   Begin by verbally describing events to another person. The questions this person asks during the conversation will help clarify and enhance the description. Practice this verbalization technique with a description of something passionate related to teaching, such as a great lesson, a child who connected with your lesson, or a great workshop you attended. Once the reflection can be clearly articulated out loud, it is time to write the description. You will probably need to write several drafts of the reflection. In the first draft, focus on writing a complete description. During the second draft, edit the reflection for clarity and for grammatical and spelling mistakes. Once you have written several reflections, the process will become easier.

Sample Description Questions	
Who was involved?	What was your role?
When did it happen?	What was the outcome?
What happened?	Where did it happen?
What are the details?	

Description Practice Prompts

Prompt One: Think about the best lesson you ever taught. Describe it. Who was involved? Where did it happen? What was the objective of the lesson? What subject was it? What happened first, second, third?
Prompt Two: Choose one of the best staff development workshops you have attended. Describe it. Why did you go? What material was covered? Who conducted the workshop? Where was it held?
Prompt Three: Think about a child impacted by your teaching. Describe him/her. Who is the child? What is he/she like? What impact did you have? What specific examples can you give about the impact?

Analysis   The process of analysis entails a critical examination of the evidence. Break it into patterns and determine the strengths and areas in which to improve. This is a difficult task for some people because they must look critically at themselves and their own work. Begin by creating a plus/delta chart that can conveniently be made from a "T" diagram. On the "plus" side, write down all the strengths of the evidence. Record areas in need of improvement on the delta side. This simple chart allows for an organized way to begin the second stage of reflection. Once the chart is completed, you can begin the first written draft of this portion of the reflection. Again, the second draft should focus on clarity and grammatical improvements.

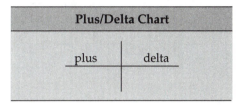

Plus/Delta Chart	
plus	delta

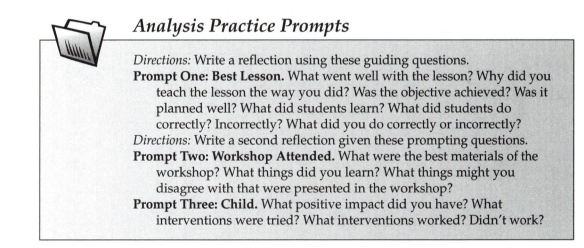

Analysis Practice Prompts

Directions: Write a reflection using these guiding questions.
Prompt One: Best Lesson. What went well with the lesson? Why did you teach the lesson the way you did? Was the objective achieved? Was it planned well? What did students learn? What did students do correctly? Incorrectly? What did you do correctly or incorrectly?
Directions: Write a second reflection given these prompting questions.
Prompt Two: Workshop Attended. What were the best materials of the workshop? What things did you learn? What things might you disagree with that were presented in the workshop?
Prompt Three: Child. What positive impact did you have? What interventions were tried? What interventions worked? Didn't work?

Planning   This component is the most important part of the reflection. If you don't address how you will use the information, then the reflection is essentially useless to you or your readers. This component of reflection emphasizes positive change in teachers' behavior and provides the intrigue for reading portfolios. A good way to begin this component of the reflection is to brainstorm impacts of the evidence. A list may include 2 or 20 items. Once the list is brainstormed, write the first draft of this section. Then, edit and rewrite until you are satisfied with the reflection.

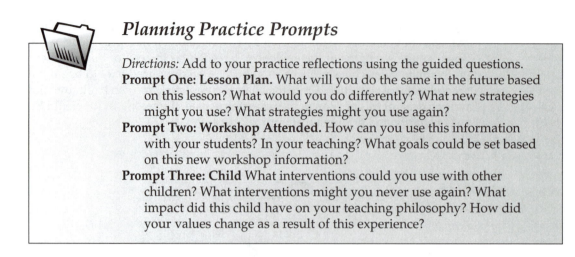

Planning Practice Prompts

Directions: Add to your practice reflections using the guided questions.
Prompt One: Lesson Plan. What will you do the same in the future based on this lesson? What would you do differently? What new strategies might you use? What strategies might you use again?
Prompt Two: Workshop Attended. How can you use this information with your students? In your teaching? What goals could be set based on this new workshop information?
Prompt Three: Child What interventions could you use with other children? What interventions might you never use again? What impact did this child have on your teaching philosophy? How did your values change as a result of this experience?

WHAT IF THIS SEEMS DIFFICULT?

One great tip is to recruit a friend to help with this process. A friend who is a teacher would be the best choice. Use this person as a peer reviewer. Even great writers have someone edit their work.

WHERE AND WHEN TO REFLECT?

It is often difficult for teachers to find time to reflect. Reflection can happen in many places at many times. It is important to reflect in a physically comfortable place. If teaching episodes are used for evidence, you should reflect on them soon after the delivery of these lessons so details are fresh and clear.

Places and times for teachers to reflect	
1. at the end of the day	3. during planning
2. in the car to and from school	4. at home

CLOSING THOUGHTS

Reflection practice develops over time. At first this might seem overwhelming and difficult, but it will become easier with time. Reflection brings a voice to portfolios—the teacher's voice. The voice makes the portfolio come to life for readers. Without reflection, a portfolio cannot tell a teacher's story.

REFERENCES

Cady, J. (1998). Teaching orientation: Teaching. *Education, 118*(3), 459–471.

McLaughlin, M., & Vogt, M. (1998). Portfolio assessment for inservice teachers: A collaborative model. In *Professional portfolio models: Applications in education.* Norwood, MA: Christopher-Gorden Publishers.

National Board for Professional Teaching Standards. (1996). *Middle childhood/generalist standards for national board certification.* Detroit: NBPTS.

Schon, D. (1987). *Educating the reflective practitioner.* San Francisco: Jossey-Bass.

Sparks-Langer, G. M., & Colton, A. B. (1991). Synthesis of research on teachers' reflective thinking. *Educational Leadership, 48*(6), 37–44.

P A R T

II

APPLICATIONS OF PORTFOLIO DEVELOPMENT

❧

❧

Now is the time to consider your specific circumstances. The chapters in this section focus on portfolios for teachers at different stages of their careers. Chapter 4 is for preservice teachers, and Chapter 5 is designed for those who want to create a teaching portfolio for job interviews. Beginning teachers should focus on Chapter 6 to learn how to develop a licensure portfolio. Experienced teachers who are interested in using portfolios as an alternative to traditional evaluations should read Chapter 7. Professionals who want to seek national board certification should turn to Chapter 8 for information. Chapter 9 provides helpful information about a technological trend, electronic portfolios. This handbook features information for teachers at every career stage.

Each chapter is organized using the same method. The standard format allows readers to go immediately to the chapter in which they are interested. Each chapter begins with an introduction, followed by the purpose and audience for each type of portfolio and organizational features. Sample evidence and assessment criteria are also identified. A general overview section is presented, along with specific examples for each type of portfolio. Guiding questions are provided to help plan portfolios.

CHAPTER 4

Portfolios for Preservice Teachers

Preservice teachers are in the first phase of their professional career, the acquisition of a license to teach. Teacher preparation occurs, for most individuals, during undergraduate preparation at a college or university. Students enrolled in teacher preparation programs create portfolios to demonstrate their knowledge, skills, and attitudes related to teaching.

Preservice teachers create portfolios for many reasons. As portfolio assessment of students has become increasingly prevalent in schools, it also has become more widely used in preservice teacher education programs (Barton & Collins, 1993). These include meeting program requirements or assembling evidence and reflections for personal growth. Many times requirements are outlined by university or college faculty, so that the portfolio's purpose is predetermined for the preservice teacher education program. Even if a program doesn't prescribe a portfolio over time, preservice teachers may choose to create a portfolio for many different reasons. Over the course of a teacher licensure program, students develop many valuable skills and complex experiences related to teaching. A portfolio can help a professional make sense out of the multitude of experiences and knowledge acquired during a program. It can bring into focus a clear picture of an individual as a growing, changing professional. Most of all, a portfolio allows one to demonstrate to others skills, knowledge, and abilities related to teaching (Campbell, Cignetti, Melenyzer, Nettles, & Wyman, 1997).

All three types of portfolios, process, product, and showcase, are useful to preservice teachers even if their education programs do not require them. The move toward performance-based assessment in teacher education programs across the nation is resulting in the requirement of portfolios in teacher education programs. Performance-based assessment, a result of standards-driven programs, requires prospective teachers to be assessed on what they know and are able to do (INTASC, 1992).

Many teachers choose to create portfolios for their own professional reasons. Preservice teachers who would like to develop their reflection skills and want to increase their professional experiences should consider creating a portfolio. Using program requirements or "outcomes" is a simple, direct way to organize a portfolio based on preservice education coursework. These "outcomes," commonly called *program goals,* are a good organizational framework for preservice teachers developing a portfolio.

All three types of portfolios can be used to show program requirements. A process portfolio can be created that shows the preservice teacher's progress in a program during different classes. Evidence can be included from each class in the program with reflections. Over the entire program, preservice teachers can create a portfolio that shows their abilities as a teacher in relation to objectives of the program or each class. Specifically, a program might have the students planning and teaching a variety of lessons. The program has field experiences in a sequence of classes over four semesters. In these field experiences, preservice teachers write lesson plans and teach them in their field sites. Students can place these lesson plans and teaching reflections from each field experience in their portfolio. In addition, the developers (students) can reflect over time on the improvements in their teaching.

Preservice Process Portfolio

Purpose: Show program requirements are met.
Sample Requirement: Writing and implementing a variety of lesson plans over a sequence of courses.
Types of Evidence: Lesson plans with reflections.
Process: A series of lesson plans are placed in the portfolio. Reflections focus on how each lesson plan was better/improved over the last one.
Product: Specific lesson plans and reflections are required for portfolio.
Showcase: Students would choose which lesson plans (or if any lesson plans) and reflections would be placed in their portfolios.

Another option is to create a showcase portfolio showing a preservice teacher's best work over the course of the program. Using the lesson plan example, preservice teachers would choose which lesson plans they would include in the portfolio. Some students might include all lesson plans while others might include only one. The key for the showcase portfolio is that each student chooses which evidence, in his/her opinion, best reflects program requirements.

A third choice would be for preservice teachers to create a product portfolio that contained specific pieces of evidence reflecting program outcomes. Again, using the lesson plan example, the program requires specific lesson plans and reflections be included in the portfolio. Each of these types of portfolios could be used for the purpose of demonstrating program requirements.

Another organizational design for a process or product portfolio model would be to use goals determined by the preservice teachers or a set of adopted standards or goals. Standards-driven portfolios are usually developed using adopted standards, such as the INTASC standards for beginning teachers.

GOALS AND STANDARDS PORTFOLIOS

Using personal or program goals or standards as an organizational framework, preservice teachers may develop a product or process portfolio to show the relationship between the goals or standards and the knowledge, skills, and abilities of a preservice teacher. If preservice teachers are demonstrating meeting the goals, a product portfolio is the best choice. Process portfolios may be used if developers want to show evidence that demonstrates how skills, knowledge, and attributes related to each goal or standard are obtained step by step.

TYPE ONE: THE GOAL-DRIVEN PRODUCT PORTFOLIO

The purpose of this product portfolio is to show that preservice teachers met the teaching goals they established. Since a developer is showing competence related to specific goals, a product portfolio would be the best choice. The audience may be themselves, other preservice teachers or university/college faculty. This type of portfolio differs from other goal-driven models because the preservice teacher determines what goals will be demonstrated in the portfolio.

Prospective teachers in the same program may have different goals. For example, one student may focus her goals on developing skills to work in a rural school. Sample goals for this portfolio might include: (1) understanding and motivating the rural child, (2) working with multiple groups in the same classroom, and (3) developing strategies that integrate art and music into the core curriculum (in many rural schools, teachers are responsible for all subjects).

Another student in the same program may focus on technology in the classroom. Sample goals for this student may be: (1) integrating technology in the classroom, (2) learning to use different types of software, and (3) facilitating student development through technology. Again, the key is that each student is responsible for setting and demonstrating attainment of each goal. Since the portfolio is personal, the goals can be unique. If you are interested in this type of portfolio, you may first want to consider what components of teaching most interest you.

Organization

The product portfolio is organized by goals. The length varies, depending on the type of goals and the audience for the portfolio. Students in a one-year teacher education program may have a smaller portfolio than those in education classes for two or three years. The portfolio is developed by preservice teachers. Professors and fellow students may provide feedback and direction about the appropriateness and direction of the portfolio.

Sample Product Portfolio Set-Up Using One Goal

Goal: To teach effectively using a variety of strategies.
Evidence: (1) lesson plans showing variety of strategies from various field experiences; (2) written observations from supervising teachers about performance from practicum experiences and student teaching; (3) long-term plan for unit taught during student teaching that shows a variety of strategies.
Organization: Three-ring binder.
Reflection: Based on question: How does evidence show goal has been met?
Assessment: Oral and written feedback from university/college faculty and fellow students.

The format is simple. Depending on the number of goals, students divide the portfolio into the same number of sections. Five goals are covered in five different sections. The evidence is gathered from classes and field experiences in the teacher education program. Developers may choose any type of evidence that is consistent with the goals.

Reflections focus on how goals are met through the evidence. Assessment may occur through written review or oral feedback from faculty members. Other types of assessment could include peer review with other students, and presentations and interviews with faculty members.

The advantages of this type of portfolio include clear, consistent goals driving the portfolio and an easy format for organization. The major disadvantage is this type of portfolio is determining the goals.

Questions to Direct Product Portfolio Development

1. *What are the goals of your program?* Sample goals include:
   - effective teaching
   - ability to manage students (classroom management)
   - hands-on instruction
   - professional growth
   - knowledge of subject matter

2. *What goals would you like to demonstrate in your portfolio?* Consider the sample goals listed previously. Are any of these goals consistent with yours in relation to teaching? What other goals do you have? Think in broad terms.

3. *What types of evidence would demonstrate each goal?* Sample evidence includes lesson plans, student work, written feedback, compositions, journals kept during practicum experiences, professional activities, and units developed.

4. *What type of physical organization would this portfolio have?* The easiest organization is a three-ring binder divided by goals.

5. *What is the role of university/college faculty?* Typically, faculty members provide informal assessment.

6. *What types of reflections would you want to see in this portfolio?* Would there be a reflection for each piece of evidence or for each goal?

Sample Goals-Driven Product Portfolio

Introduction: Kelly Cave is a student in a preservice middle grades program. She will work with students in grades six through nine when she graduates. She is enrolled in a small two-year teacher education program. During these two years, she has been in two practicum experiences and a semester-long student teaching experience. In addition, she has been in a series of middle level coursework.

Many of Kelly's goals reflect program goals:
1. plan lessons and units that match the state curriculum and meet needs of adolescents
2. integrate curriculum using two or more subjects
3. plan activities for adolescents that meet physical and psychosocial developmental needs
4. develop classroom management strategies
5. be involved in professional activities

Developer   Kelly (preservice teacher)

Purpose   To demonstrate goals are met

Organization   Three-ring binder, organized by goals

Teacher's Story*   *I organized my portfolio by each goal. For organizational reasons, I bought a big notebook and a set of dividers. I kept all of my assignments and practicum information in a big cardboard box during the semester. In addition, I would write notes on each piece of evidence to include in my reflection. At the end*

---

*Reprinted with permission. Kelly Cave is now a successful teacher at Gentry Middle School in Surry County, North Carolina.

of each semester, I would choose evidence to place under each goal. It was important for me to balance what I learned in class with my practicum experiences in the public schools. As I worked on my portfolio, I began to see the "big picture" of what I believed, knew, and would do as a teacher. This was an important assignment, in my opinion, because it forced me to reflect on what I had learned and to take charge or organizing my thoughts and skills as a middle level teacher.

How did I organize it?   *I began by setting up my portfolio in my binder. As mentioned previously, I used the "pile" method of organization by keeping all assignments and practicum paperwork in a cardboard box in the corner of my room. I would drop everything into the box when I got it back from the professor.*

What evidence did I include?   *In the front of the portfolio I placed a cover page that included my name, major, and a piece of clip art. Next came an organizational table of contents. My **first section** was an **introduction of myself** where I placed my resume and autobiography that I wrote in one of my classes. Following this were the five goals divided into sections.*

Order of Introductory Evidence

1. Cover page
2. Table of Contents
3. *Introduction Section*
    a. Resume
    b. Autobiography
4. *Goals by Sections*

Goals and Evidence

Goal 1: To plan lessons and units that match the state curriculum and meet needs of adolescents.

Evidence: *A copy of the state curriculum, five different lesson plans with correlated state goal and objectives (the plans also reflect five different methods that are appropriate to use with adolescents), unit plan (long range), video tape of myself teaching three of the lessons.*

Goal 2: To integrate curriculum using two or more subjects.

Evidence: *Integrated unit prepared for methods class, integrated unit taught during student teaching experience, samples of student work of integrated assignments from unit, informal surveys from students about integrated unit.*

Goal 3: To plan activities for adolescents that meet physical and psychosocial developmental needs

Evidence: *Intramural plan for students, observation of exploratory courses done in practicum, advisor-advisee curriculum (planned) and activities taught during student teaching, case study of adolescent done during the first year.*

Goal 4: To develop classroom management strategies.

Evidence: *Series of case studies done in course work, semester-long observation record of class behavior, management plan for class, log of management record during student teaching, preliminary classroom rules, and procedures for first year of teaching.*

Goal 5: To involve themselves in professional development activities.

Evidence: *Agenda from student middle school association meeting, list of professional organizations that I belong to, list of workshops attended during my student teaching experience, copy of PTA membership card.*

A Moment to Think

1. Choose a goal. Divide a piece of paper into two columns.
2. In the left column, brainstorm for two minutes about course assignments and school experiences you have done.
3. Now, move to the right column. For each item in the left column, give a reason it fits under the goal you have chosen. This part of the activity will help you with your reflection section.

Author's Reaction to Evidence

Kelly's evidence is appropriate for each goal. Obviously, she needs to choose her evidence carefully to avoid repetition. For example, lesson plans can go under goals one and two, so Kelly must decide which type of plans she should put where. While readers might disagree with her organizational decisions, the point to remember is that placing the evidence is her choice. The keys to a successful goals-oriented portfolio are the selection of appropriate evidence and clear reflections that support the work samples.

Reflection

A short reflection is written to describe each piece of evidence and to tell how it meets the goal. For each section, Kelly writes a longer cumulative reflection that encompasses all evidence and its relevance. In the longer reflection, Kelly also focuses on what she learned and how she would apply it to her teaching philosophy.

Sample Short Reflection for Goal 1
Evidence: copy of state curriculum

This is a copy of the math curriculum for our state. It is expected that I will teach the content of this curriculum in sixth grade. I have included this under goal one because it shows that I understand there is a state curriculum that I am to follow when planning lesson plans and units.

Assessment   *At the end of the first year, I asked for informal feedback about my portfolio. There were three categories in which written feedback was given by faculty members: (1) content, (2) reflections, and (3) organization and general feedback. Based on the feedback I received for the first year, I revised my portfolio for the second year. This interim feedback was valuable for me; it allowed me to see that I was on the right track.*

At the end of the second year, I had the option to present my portfolio to a group of peers and university faculty. I used the evidence from each goal in a 20-minute presentation to summarize how I met each goal, and then I answered questions. This was a powerful experience. I had to take everything I had done over two years and summarize it. This experience made me think about each goal individually and how to link them together. I really reflected on everything that I had put together over the two-year period. I reread all of my reflections and wrote a summary based on all of them. I didn't get a grade on my portfolio. I did it for myself. I would not trade this opportunity for any other.

Author's Reaction

This type of portfolio allows for personal growth on the part of the preservice teacher. By the time Kelly was finished with her portfolio, she understood herself better and grew as a teacher as a result of this experience. The most valuable outcome is her ability to reflect on her experiences.

TYPE TWO: THE STANDARDS PORTFOLIO

A standards portfolio in preservice teacher education is developed using a set of standards as the organizational guide. Any type of standards can be used to develop a portfolio. These standards can be from the INTASC or chosen from any national organization such as the National Middle School Association or the National Council for Teachers of Mathematics. The majority of teaching organizations have developed standards. These can be readily organized and assessed.

In this chapter, the INTASC standards have been chosen because they outline good teaching principles for any teacher at any career stage. Any set of standards can replace them and the same portfolio organizational pattern can be used.

INTASC Standards

The INTASC standards were developed by a group of educators from states across the nation who belong to the Interstate New Teacher Assessment and Support Consortium under the auspices of the Council of Chief State School Officers. The purpose of these standards is to assess the knowledge, skills, and abilities of beginning teachers. In 1987, the Council of Chief State School Officers established a consortium to enhance collaboration among states interested in rethinking teacher assessment for initial licensing and for preparation and induction into the profession. This consortium came about as a result of restructuring efforts for America's schools. High school graduates are being required to perform at higher levels in the workforce, thus demanding changes in the curriculum. Rather than merely "covering the curriculum," teachers are expected to find ways to support and connect with the needs of all learners. These learner-centered approaches to teaching require change in teacher licensure, the vehicle for providing consistency in the type of teacher who enters the classroom. The INTASC standards have been adopted in more than 17 states as a consistent measure for teacher licensure and competency (INTASC, 1992).

Preservice teacher programs have adopted the INTASC standards for two reasons: (1) NCATE, the accreditation organization for schools of education, has incorporated the INTASC standards into its outcomes, and (2) schools of education want to prepare their students by using the standards for beginning teachers

Confronting INTASC

© Thomson 2000

since this is the outcome of teacher preparation programs. Following is a description of the standards, with specific indicators outlined for each as adopted by the consortium. The authors provide sample evidence for each standard.

Describing the Standards

Standard One: Content Pedagogy   *The teacher understands the central concepts, tools of inquiry, and structure of the discipline(s) he or she teaches and can create learning experiences that make these aspects of subject matter meaningful to students.*

Evidence should show   Instruction is consistent with state curriculum guidelines, curriculum is supplemented with external resources, methods of inquiry are used, and the central concepts and tools of inquiry of the discipline are evident in planning.

Sample Evidence
- lesson plans with correlation to state curriculum showing external resources: *lesson plans that show state curriculum goals and objectives and/or district goals*
- units of study (integrated, interdisciplinary): *series of lesson plans around a central topic, concept, or theme that show connections between different subjects around the central focus*
- inquiry lesson plans: *lessons that are built around a central question with the teacher planning the role of facilitator; students are not told answers, but are led to them through experiences*

Standard Two: Student Development   *The teacher understands how children learn and develop, and can provide learning opportunities that support their intellectual, social, and personal development.*

Evidence should show   Evidence you can plan/assess linking to students' prior knowledge, encouragement of reflection on prior knowledge and its connection to new information, integration of learning with other disciplines or real-world experiences, experiences for students that are appropriate for the social, emotional, and cognitive development of students, and providing opportunities for learners to be responsible for learning.

Sample Evidence
- lesson plans: *any subject*
- manipulatives used: *tangible items used to explain concepts specifically used in mathematics*
- photos: *of students, activities, groupwork*
- developmental checklist: *showing growth of students against developmental criteria in different areas, usually done in early childhood programs*
- varied strategies used (lesson plans and units): *lesson plans and handouts visualizing types of teacher and learner strategies used in the classroom*

- floor plans of classroom: *a graphic representation of how the classroom is set up, including desks, learning centers, bulletin boards, etc.*

Standard Three: Diverse Learners   *The teacher understands how students differ in their approaches to learning and creates instructional opportunities that are adapted to diverse learners.*

Evidence should show   Adaptations of instruction to meet the needs of varying learner styles, strengths, and needs of learners (time and circumstance of work, tasks assigned, communication modes), and incorporation of cultural contexts within community.

Sample Evidence
- differentiated lesson plans: *plans showing how assignments and strategies are changed or extended to meet the needs of all learners*
- videos of student performances: *videotapes of speeches, projects, and participation of students*
- learning centers: *self-managed work centers set up around tables or desks where students investigate in a particular area*
- bulletin boards: *artistic work on a theme on a flat wallboard*

Standard Four: Critical Thinking   *The teacher understands and uses a variety of instructional strategies to encourage students' development of critical thinking, problem solving, and performance skills.*

Evidence should show   Use of multiple teaching strategies for challenging critical thinking (questioning activities), demonstration of how students are encouraged to identify learning resources, and use of multiple instructional strategies (facilitator, coach, instructor, audience).

Sample Evidence
- video: *showing higher order questioning, activities, and assessments*
- explanation of grouping procedures: *write-up explaining levels in the classroom and how critical thinking is done with all students*
- collection of pre- and post-test data: *test data showing how students did prior to and after a lesson, concept, skill, or unit is taught*
- planning based on students' differentiated abilities: *lesson plans showing how all students' needs are met*

Standard Five: Motivation and Management   *The teacher encourages an understanding of individual and group motivation and behavior to create a learning environment that encourages positive social interactions, active engagement in learning, and self-motivation.*

Evidence should show   Procedures and rules for classroom management, ability to organize and manage time, space, and activities conducive to learning, ability to analyze and adjust classroom environment to enhance social relationships, student motivation/engagement and ways students are organized for various types of instruction, such as small and large groups and cooperative learning.

Sample Evidence

- management plan: *classroom rules and consequences*
- incentive system: *student rewards*
- parent communication: *letters, notes, phone calls, progress reports, and other ways parents are contacted*
- cooperative activities: *lesson plans and pictures that show how students work together in cooperative ways*
- classroom procedures: *how papers are turned in, pencils sharpened, questions answered, and other general processes*

Standard Six: Communication and Technology   *The teacher uses knowledge of effective verbal, nonverbal, and media communication techniques to foster active inquiry, collaboration, and supportive interaction in the classroom.*

Evidence should show   Ability to model effective, culturally sensitive communication, support of learner expression (speaking, writing, and other media) and use of a variety of media communication tools to enrich instruction/learning.

Sample Evidence

- video: *teaching showing motivation and communication*
- student evaluations: *information from students about classroom environment and teaching*
- lesson plans showing uses of technology: *lessons showing technology as a teaching or learning strategy*
- communication to parents and students: *written documents such as a syllabi and letters to and from parents*

Standard Seven: Planning   *The teacher plans instruction based upon knowledge of subject matter, students, the community, and curriculum goals.*

Evidence should show   Long-range units and daily lesson plans based on curriculum goals, adjusted plans based on unanticipated sources of input or learner needs, and appropriate plans for curriculum goals, diverse learners, and problem solving.

Sample Evidence

- short-term and long-term objectives: *specific outcomes for each day, week, month, or year*
- pacing guide: *outline of what is taught and when throughout the school year*
- unit plans: *a series of lessons around a central theme or concept*

Standard Eight: Assessment   *The teacher understands and uses formal and informal assessment strategies to evaluate and ensure the continuous intellectual, social, and physical development of the learner.*

Evidence should show   Use of a variety of assessment strategies, use of assessment strategies to adapt and adjust instruction, acquisition of information about students' learning behavior, learning needs, and the students themselves, useful records of student work and performance, and demonstrations of involving learners in self-assessment to inform them of strengths/needs and to encourage goal setting.

Sample Evidence
- formal tests: *standardized test scores for class or school*
- work samples: *student work showing variety of students' abilities and types of assessments used in the class*
- writing samples: *student writing*
- authentic work products: *projects, products, and other real-life work by students*
- records of student and parent conferences: *logs, records, team logs of conferences*

Standard Nine: Professional Development   *The teacher is a reflective practitioner who continually evaluates the effects of his/her choices and actions on others (students, parents, and other professionals in the learning community) and who actively seeks out opportunities to grow professionally.*

Evidence should show   Evaluation of self and self-improvement.

Sample Evidence
- attendance at professional meetings/presentations: *programs, handouts, or materials received at professional meetings*
- attendance at workshops: *staff development agendas*
- articles read/reviewed: *summary of articles read, especially with ideas that are implemented*
- committee work: *listing of committee participation in school*
- volunteer hours: *work done with students on "own time" and other contributions to the school and community, beyond regular day*
- journals: *personal journal about teaching experience*

Standard Ten: School/Community Involvement   *The teacher fosters relationships with school colleagues, parents, and agencies in the larger community to support students' learning and well-being.*

Evidence should show   Documentation of participation in school activities, communication with parents, and consultations with other professionals on behalf of students.

Sample Evidence
- home visits: *logs or records of home visits*
- knowledge of community agencies: *summaries or explanations of links between agencies and students/schools*
- parent communication: *sample letters, logs*

Developing an INTASC Portfolio

The purpose of this portfolio is for preservice teachers to show they have the knowledge, skills, and abilities to teach successfully as outlined in the INTASC standards. The developers are teacher education students. These students may

FIGURE 4–1   Whitney Lawrence, student intern, confers with her
clinical intern, Linda Freeman, about her portfolio.

get university/college faculty to serve as codevelopers. The audience is varied
depending on the purpose of the portfolio. It can include university/college
faculty or the preservice teacher. It is organized by the 10 standards. Reflection
emphasizes a description of evidence that shows how standards are met and
the impact on students' development. Assessment can be done in a variety of
ways, both formally and informally. Interviews, written reflections, peer reviews, presentations, and blind reviews can be used. Informal interviews and
feedback with university/college faculty members and the students' peers can
only strengthen the portfolio process.

Questions to Direct Standards Portfolio Development

1. What standards would you adopt?
2. What role will your professor and/or adviser play in the development of
   the portfolio?
3. Over what time period will portfolio be developed? One semester? One
   year? Two years?

The following sample shows how a university department adopted an
INTASC Standards organizational design. Individual preservice teachers
could adopt this model or use a more general design where they show how
standards are met throughout their program. One option would be to create a
standards portfolio during the student teaching experience.

Process Portfolio Design Using the INTASC Standards

The East Carolina University elementary and middle grades department has adopted a process INTASC portfolio model. The portfolio documents the development of preservice teachers against the INTASC standards over a 2½-year period. The faculty chose the portfolio as one means of assessing students because it is a type of authentic assessment that allows students to illustrate their learning through multiple forms of evidence and to reflect on it. The portfolio is seen as a working document that preservice teachers can build on as they move into their professional life as educators.

Purposes of Portfolio   This department has three purposes:
1. To be a vehicle for thoughtful and knowledgeable reflection on the relationship between the preservice teacher's work and the INTASC standards.
2. To demonstrate growth of knowledge and skills that lead to effective teaching. These will be presented in the form of evidence categorized by the INTASC standards.
3. To further understand portfolio processes and applications.

Organization   A process portfolio shows growth over time. During the 2½ years students are in the program, the focus is on development of a process portfolio that shows the preservice teachers' growth in the profession over their time in the program. Each student keeps a portfolio in a three-ring binder and begins it in the sophomore year. The portfolio culminates in the senior year.

Developer(s)   Preservice teachers with assistance from faculty in the department.

Audience   University faculty.

Reflection   Students write reflections for each piece of evidence. They describe the evidence and its relevance to the INTASC standard and detail how it impacts their teaching.

Assessment   At the end of each of the five semesters (second semester sophomore to second semester senior) students turn in the portfolio to one instructor whose assignment is predetermined. A tracking sheet is kept in the portfolio and informal feedback is given to the student each semester. A minimum of five pieces of evidence is required for each standard by the end of the program. The portfolio counts as a participation grade (approximately 10 percent) in each class. At the end of the senior year, after the student teaching experience, students turn in their portfolios for a final review. A two-way conversation is held between the university supervisor and the preservice teacher.

Evidence   The one criteria for the portfolio is that students include a variety of evidence. They are required to include a wide range of media. As students move through the sequence of classes, different INTASC stan-

Middle Grades Education Sample Course Sequence Correlation with INTASC Standard

Course	Class/Semester	Standard(s)
Introduction to Major	Sophomore second semester	Introduction to Standards
Introduction to Pre-Adolescence & Middle School	Junior first semester	1, 2, 3, 4, & 9
Curriculum and Strategies	Junior second semester	1, 2, 3, 4, 7, & 9
Classroom Management, Curriculum and Assessment	Senior first semester	1, 2, 3, 4, 5, 6, 7, 8, 9, & 10
Internship/Student Teaching	Senior second semester	All

dards are naturally emphasized. This helps students include evidence from each standard.

Now you can review a student sample using this organization.

Sample INTASC Student Process Portfolio

Introduction   Russell Vernon is a student in a large middle level teacher education program. He will teach in grades six through nine when he graduates. He is in the last semester of his program (second semester senior). Two and one half years ago, he began his INTASC portfolio in his first major course. Over the span of five semesters, he has turned in his portfolio five times for informal reviews.

Standards Used: INTASC

Developers   Preservice teacher

Purpose   For preservice teachers to demonstrate they meet the INTASC standards

Organization   All students organize their portfolios by the 10 standards. Each student in the program is expected to divide a three-ring binder into 10 sections. Developers decide what evidence to include in the portfolio, but a minimum of five pieces are added each semester.

Teacher's Story*   *During my first education course, we were introduced to the INTASC portfolio model. At first, I was overwhelmed. Even though the instructor*

---

*Reprinted with permission. Russell Vernon is now a successful teacher in Rockingham County, North Carolina.

did a good job introducing the concept, I didn't know what to expect the first time I turned in my portfolio. I was very anxious about the feedback that I would receive. After my portfolio was reviewed, I was glad that feedback was given. The next semester we added five more pieces of evidence. This time I felt more confident when I turned in my portfolio. In my senior year, my portfolio went through a major transformation. I began to get really serious about what I was adding and how it would look to potential employers. During this phase, I pulled out much of the evidence that I had added earlier in my program and replaced it with samples collected during my internship [student teaching]. Overall, I feel compiling the portfolio is a great experience for preservice teachers. I learned that I had the skills and abilities to be a good teacher, and I could see the growth I made over the two and one half years.

How Did I Organize It? *I was required to set it up by the 10 standards. This was easy to do. I chose evidence as I went through the courses and added it to my portfolio. Once I made a decision to add something, I went ahead and put it in my binder [portfolio]. I am a linear person, so this system worked for me.*

What Evidence Did I Include? *Before the 10 standards, I had a creative cover sheet with my name and major and on the second page, a resume. In front of each divider, I wrote out the entire standard.*

Evidence
Standard 1: *team simulation demonstration that shows intern working on an interdisciplinary team, shadow study, and journal entries*
Standard 2: *media analysis collage (impact of media on adolescents), classroom environmental study, journal entries, case study*
Standard 3: *concept web, adolescent profile, lesson plans showing different strategies*
Standard 4: *team simulation, interactive bulletin board, integrated unit, videotape, photos of students in cooperative learning groups*
Standard 5: *classroom rules, description and analysis of different discipline problems during internship, classroom procedures, philosophy of management (essay)*
Standard 6: *letter to parents during internship, journal entries, phone log, project assigned with directions (to parents and students), parent conference summary sheet, technology assignments (with disk) done for class at East Carolina University*
Standard 7: *long-term planning guide, lesson plans, plan book, unit goals, objectives, and rationale taught during internship*
Standard 8: *pre- and post-test data, tests, projects, student work, and copy of grade sheet*
Standard 9: *journal entries, supervising teacher feedback sheet, dialogue journal used during internship*
Standard 10: *committees served on during internship, conferences attended during two and one half years (agenda), workshop agendas*

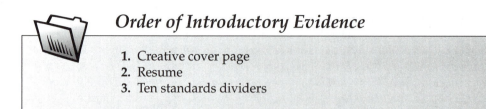

Order of Introductory Evidence

1. Creative cover page
2. Resume
3. Ten standards dividers

Author's Reaction to Evidence

Russell did a good job using a variety of media in his portfolio, including a videotape, photographs, and various assignments from courses and school experiences. He could have more evidence showing his knowledge of content, which is crucial for a middle level teacher.

Reflection   *For each piece of evidence, I wrote a reflection. In these brief reflections, I would show the connection to the INTASC standards and give a brief description of the evidence. In addition, through two presentations, I was required to summarize my beliefs about teaching.*

Sample Reflection

Evidence: Adolescent Profile Written: First semester, junior year (second semester of portfolio development)
Reflection: *This entry was placed under standard three because it proves that I have acquired an understanding of how students differ in their approaches to learning and the changes that occur during the adolescent years. This assignment helped me prepare for the future as I venture into the middle schools.*

Assessment   At the end of every semester for five semesters, I was given informal feedback about my portfolio. In my senior year, I was required to present my portfolio twice (at the end of both semesters). By this point, I was ready to present my evidence and respond to questions about my beliefs, knowledge, and skills. These opportunities allowed me to really think about what I believe and, also, what I would say in an interview. The portfolio was a requirement in the program. Each semester, it was given a participation grade using a checklist, and during my internship semester it was a requirement. If I had not completed it, I would have received a lower grade in my internship.

Author's Reaction

This type of portfolio allows for personal and professional growth. University faculty could use the portfolio evidence to review program outcomes and the effectiveness of their teaching majors. The entire process allows for confidence building in students and reflection time for faculty.

ASSESSMENT

One of the most important areas to take into consideration when developing a portfolio is to consider how it will be assessed. Preservice teachers may face a variety of assessment methods. If portfolios are developed for personal reasons, no assessment methods will be used. Individuals who are developing them as part of a program requirement will have them assessed.

Assessment Methods

Interview   A popular method of assessing portfolios is a one-on-one or small group student interview. During this allotted time, developers present key evidence that shows major components of the portfolio. If it is a standards portfolio, developers should be prepared to outline how each standard is met. Preparing for the interview is quite easy. Developers should review their portfolio so they are familiar with the location of different components and the content. Sample interview questions include: What have you learned in this program? What does the portfolio show about your teaching? How did you show standard X or goal Y is met? What are your strengths? What areas do you still need to improve in? This is a time-consuming method for teacher education faculty.

Presentations   A twist on the one-on-one interview, the presentation is usually made to faculty and peers. Given an allotted amount of time, developers should be prepared to present an overview of their program giving highlights from different sections. Overheads or visuals may be helpful to facilitate this process. In the presentation, students are generally asked to give an

FIGURE 4–2   Whitney Lawrence, student intern, reviews evidence for her professional portfolio.

overview, lasting 10 to 30 minutes. The end of the presentation is usually a time for questions from the audience. Be prepared to answer specific questions about evidence presented, your strengths, areas to improve, and skills and knowledge learned throughout the program.

Written Evaluation Another option is a written reflection that summarizes the contents of the portfolio or analyzes your views about the documents or process. This method allows one to be reflective and in-depth about feelings, views, and artifacts in the portfolio. An excellent method to encourage written expression and reflection, it might be combined with one of the above methods. Write honestly and ask someone to proofread your work if this component is required.

Checklists and Rubrics If developed for a grade, checklists or rubrics may be one of the assessment methods. Specific criteria related to purposes of the portfolio will be outlined and students' abilities to meet these criteria will be judged. Many times, rubrics or scoring criteria will be completed during the last assessment of a process portfolio, after many informal assessments. Checklists provide developers with specific information about their ability to meet evaluation criteria.

CLOSING THOUGHTS

In this chapter, descriptions and samples of goal-driven product and standards portfolios were presented. Preservice teachers who want to create a portfolio can use this chapter as a guide. Teacher education faculty may wish to use these guidelines to create a portfolio design for their students.

REFERENCES

Barton, J., & Collins, A. (1993). Portfolios in teacher education. *Journal of Teacher Education, 44*(33), 200–209.

Campbell, D. M., Cignetti, P. B., Melenyzer, B. J., Nettles, D. H., & Wyman, R. M., Jr. (1997). *How to develop a professional portfolio: A manual for teachers.* Boston: Allyn and Bacon.

Interstate New Teacher Assessment and Support Consortium. (1992). *Model standards for beginning teacher licensing and development: A resource for state dialogue.* Washington, DC: Council of Chief State School Officers.

C H A P T E R

5

Portfolios for Getting a Job

Many teachers use a portfolio to help secure a teaching position. In metropolitan areas where jobs are competitive, the portfolio can be the ticket a teacher needs to get a desirable position. The job portfolio is different from those created at other stages of a teaching career because it is designed specifically for an external audience, one that will make a career decision based on its contents and other criteria. The portfolio is taken on a job interview at the district office and the school level. The number of success stories of teaching candidates who use portfolios to secure positions multiplies each year (Hurst & Wilson, 1998). The marketability of potential candidates has changed in the last 15 years due to the influx of technology. Vitas, portfolios, and web pages have become more of the norm rather than the exception when searching for a desirable position.

Sample Product Portfolio

Organized by responsibilities:
Teaching second grade: sample units, class activities, strategies, classroom management plan, sample student work for this grade level
Contributing to school: work on previous committees, grade levels or collaboration with other teachers
Professional development: certificates from conferences attended, development plan, memberships in professional organizations

Danielson (1996) states, "When a teacher wants to move to a professionally more rewarding or more challenging position, the teacher must document excellence." One way to do this is through the portfolio. Portfolios are vivid visual representations of a teacher. Most would agree that interviews alone are inadequate for communicating the full range of a teacher's abilities. Used as a supplement in a job interview, the portfolio can provide evidence of a teacher's knowledge, skills, and disposition about education. Cook and Kessler (1993) assert that portfolios can be used as a tool, which, in addition to teaching credentials, allow candidates to market themselves effectively. The portfolio allows teachers to show who they are and what they believe through concrete evidence.

THE OPTIONS

Two types of portfolios are appropriate to use when searching for a job: the product and showcase portfolios (see Chapter 2 for more information). You can decide which of these to use based on your knowledge of the desired position. If you know the grade level, school, educational philosophy, and other information about the school, then you can design a product portfolio. It should contain evidence that demonstrates your specific knowledge, skills, and abilities related to specific job responsibilities. Choose the evidence with the job qualifications in mind. Establish organizational categories based on job responsibilities. For each category write a reflection. In these reflections, talk about how each category relates to the specific job and how the evidence shows your qualifications for the position. In other words, each reflection must demonstrate your ability and commitment to do the job well.

Sample Showcase Portfolio

For a high school science position, include:
Teaching beliefs: written statement about teaching philosophy
Teaching: excellent biology unit, lab lesson plans and write-ups, lesson plans showing differentiated assignments
Classroom management: classroom rules, diagram of classroom, motivation strategies
Professional development: goals for future, professional conferences attended, memberships in professional organizations

While the product portfolio is an excellent choice, most prospective teachers don't know which grade level or even which school in which they will interview. Thus, a showcase portfolio might be a better choice. Remember, in a showcase portfolio you choose your best work to demonstrate your abilities, knowledge, and dispositions. This type of portfolio can be organized by standards or domains (see Chapters 2, 4, and 7). Under each standard or domain, place your "best" works. The reflection for each standard or domain should show your knowledge, abilities, and disposition. Frameworks, discussed in Chapter 7, can be used to set up a job-seeking portfolio. If you want to develop a technology-driven product, review Chapter 9.

EVIDENCE TO INCLUDE

Some components should be included in all portfolios used for job searches. To find out what types of evidence had the greatest impact, the authors contacted the potential audience for this portfolio, principals and personnel directors. Our survey found principals and teachers on interview teams at the school level were more interested in reviewing the portfolio than the administrators at central offices. We also found that the portfolio can "break a tie" between two candidates who seem equal. Cole (1991) found portfolios give teacher candidates a competitive edge over other candidates with equal credentials.

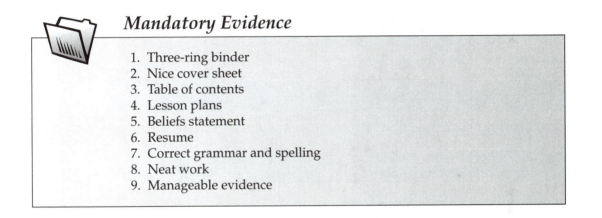

Mandatory Evidence

1. Three-ring binder
2. Nice cover sheet
3. Table of contents
4. Lesson plans
5. Beliefs statement
6. Resume
7. Correct grammar and spelling
8. Neat work
9. Manageable evidence

Finally, the principals and personnel directors identified a few components that were mandatory in the portfolio. Put the portfolio in a three-ring binder so it's easy to view. A nice, colorful cover sheet should announce your name and licensure area(s). A user-friendly table of contents should direct readers to domains or sections. Include sample lesson plans and units in the portfolio. Student learning should be the main consideration when compiling the portfolio. Include a beliefs statement or teaching philosophy and a resume. Make sure your evidence is grammatically correct and free of misspellings. Make it neat and manageable: Don't include every piece of evidence collected for the last 6 years. Be selective. Figures 5–1, 5–2, and 5–3 feature samples of a cover sheet, table of contents, and resume.

Careful consideration of contents and creative displays add value to a job portfolio. It is important to review the essential components of a portfolio presented in Chapter 2 (purpose, audience, evidence, and reflections). If you are preparing a portfolio for job interviewing or promotion only, adhere to the "less is better" adage. A cumbersome, thick portfolio may not be appealing to potential principals or interview teams.

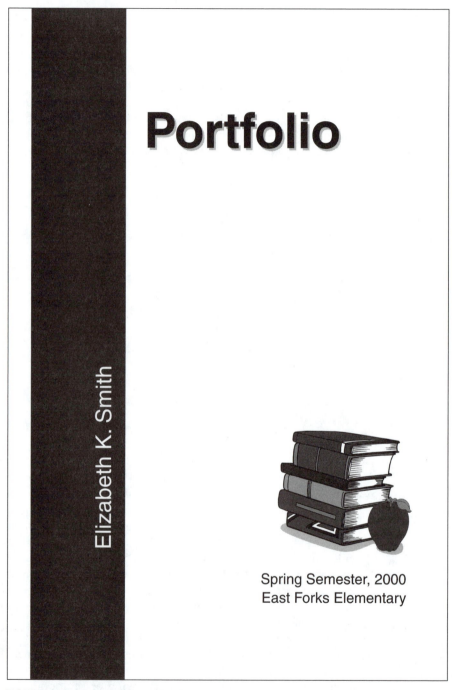

FIGURE 5-1   Sample Cover Sheet

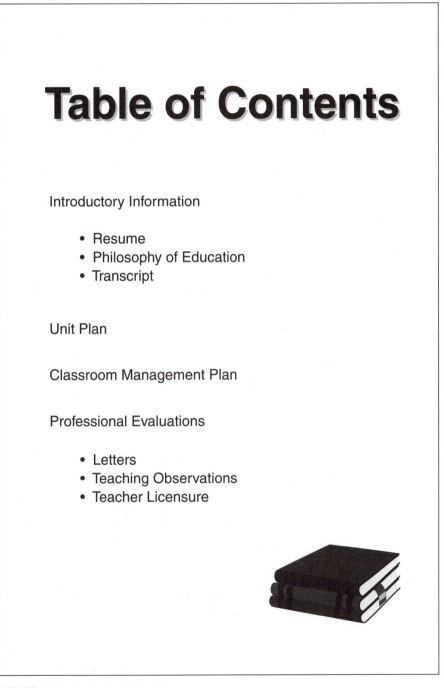

Table of Contents

Introductory Information

- Resume
- Philosophy of Education
- Transcript

Unit Plan

Classroom Management Plan

Professional Evaluations

- Letters
- Teaching Observations
- Teacher Licensure

FIGURE 5-2   Sample Table of Contents

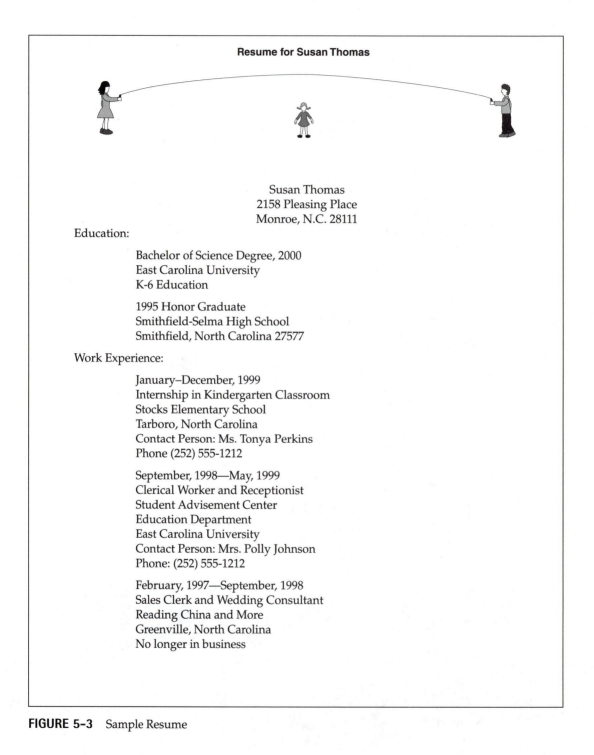

Resume for Susan Thomas

Susan Thomas
2158 Pleasing Place
Monroe, N.C. 28111

Education:

Bachelor of Science Degree, 2000
East Carolina University
K-6 Education

1995 Honor Graduate
Smithfield-Selma High School
Smithfield, North Carolina 27577

Work Experience:

January–December, 1999
Internship in Kindergarten Classroom
Stocks Elementary School
Tarboro, North Carolina
Contact Person: Ms. Tonya Perkins
Phone (252) 555-1212

September, 1998—May, 1999
Clerical Worker and Receptionist
Student Advisement Center
Education Department
East Carolina University
Contact Person: Mrs. Polly Johnson
Phone: (252) 555-1212

February, 1997—September, 1998
Sales Clerk and Wedding Consultant
Reading China and More
Greenville, North Carolina
No longer in business

FIGURE 5–3   Sample Resume

January, 1996—February, 1997
Waitress
Annabelle's Restaurant
Greenville, North Carolina
No longer in business

Summer of 1996
Sales Clerk
Royal Doulton China
Smithfield, North Carolina

Summer of 1994, 1995
Lifeguard and Swimming Instructor
Smithfield Family Pool
Contact Person: Mr. Tommy Austin

References:

Ms. Tonya Perkins
Principal
3710 Cancion Street
Tarboro Elementary School
Rocky Mount, N.C. 26858
252-555-1212
Mrs. Ethel Warner
University Supervisor
1000 College Lane
Greenville, N.C. 27858
252-555-1212
Mrs. Polly Perkins
Work Supervisor
Annabelle's Restaurant
Greenville, N.C.
252-555-1212

e-mail me! Stmail@mailprogram.net

FIGURE 5-3   Sample Resume—continued

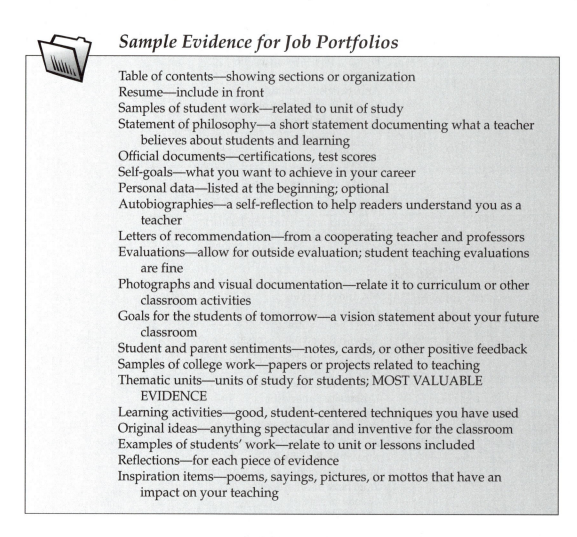

Sample Evidence for Job Portfolios

Table of contents—showing sections or organization
Resume—include in front
Samples of student work—related to unit of study
Statement of philosophy—a short statement documenting what a teacher
    believes about students and learning
Official documents—certifications, test scores
Self-goals—what you want to achieve in your career
Personal data—listed at the beginning; optional
Autobiographies—a self-reflection to help readers understand you as a
    teacher
Letters of recommendation—from a cooperating teacher and professors
Evaluations—allow for outside evaluation; student teaching evaluations
    are fine
Photographs and visual documentation—relate it to curriculum or other
    classroom activities
Goals for the students of tomorrow—a vision statement about your future
    classroom
Student and parent sentiments—notes, cards, or other positive feedback
Samples of college work—papers or projects related to teaching
Thematic units—units of study for students; MOST VALUABLE
    EVIDENCE
Learning activities—good, student-centered techniques you have used
Original ideas—anything spectacular and inventive for the classroom
Examples of students' work—relate to unit or lessons included
Reflections—for each piece of evidence
Inspiration items—poems, sayings, pictures, or mottos that have an
    impact on your teaching

THE JOB INTERVIEW

Take your portfolio to all job interviews, including those at the central office
and school level. Inform interviewers of the portfolio, but don't "push" it on
them. Most principals and teachers will review it. Usually, a principal will review it for 10 minutes while an interview team of teachers will allot approximately 30 minutes to view the portfolio. Another choice will be for the teacher
to use it to answer interview questions. For example, if you are asked what
type of teaching strategies you use, open the portfolio and point out several
lessons that incorporate different techniques. This tactic will demonstrate your

ability to "talk the talk and walk the walk." A word of caution: you must know your portfolio well to do this. It doesn't look good to fumble through a portfolio looking for something during a 30-minute interview. Another choice would be to leave the portfolio for a day so it can be reviewed.

CLOSING THOUGHTS

Portfolios are useful when interviewing for a job. The evidence allows teachers to show their knowledge, skills, and abilities. Teachers who create portfolios for this purpose are viewed as organized and productive. Those individuals who interview potential teachers view the portfolio as a way to see who best meets the qualifications for the job and who will be successful in a particular school or district. Finally, the portfolio gives credence to a teacher's beliefs and actions. This credence can get you the job you want.

REFERENCES

Cole, D., Lasley, T., Ryan, C., Swanigan, H., Tillman, B., and Uphoff, J. (1991). Developing reflection in educational course work via the professional portfolio. *GATEways to Teacher Education, 4*, 10.

Cook, D., & Kessler, J. (1993) The professional teaching portfolio: A useful tool for an effective job search. *ASCUS Annual, 15.*

Danielson, C. (1996). *Enhancing professional practice: A framework for teaching.* Alexandria, VA: Association for Supervision and Curriculum Development.

Hurst, B., & Wilson, C. (1998). Professional teaching portfolios. *Phi Delta Kappan, 79*(8), 578–583.

CHAPTER 6

Portfolios for Continuing Licensure

In Chapter 1 we discussed how portfolios enable teachers to take ownership and responsibility for their evaluations. Just as in other professions, it is the responsibility of teachers to demonstrate in their portfolios essential teaching competence using the standards developed and approved by their local school systems or states. It is also their responsibility to demonstrate their requisite knowledge, skills, and attitudes before receiving a license. This chapter deals with the portfolio as a performance-based product to evaluate beginning teachers as they move forward to a continuing license or certification.

There is a difference between a portfolio and a product. The portfolio is a collection of items teachers select for inclusion to demonstrate their competence as a teacher. The product has a collection of evidence prescribed by the agency that will assess it based upon the standards and activities identified by the school system or state. For example, required evidence could be: a 15-minute video, 10 consecutive lesson plans, two assessment measures, and three case studies to accompany activities related to instruction.

The performance-based portfolio process recognizes the very different contexts in which teachers work and provides them the autonomy to present that which best reflects their knowledge and skill in that context. The performance-based product (PBP) is a collection of evidence produced during the normal course of teaching. According to Ken Wolf (1991), it is a means of "storing and displaying evidence of a teacher's knowledge and skills." The PBP, unlike more traditional means of assessment, can reflect the richness and complexity of teaching over extended periods of time. By selecting multiple sources of evidence in authentic settings and compiling them over time, teachers can focus and reflect on the products of their teaching and their students' learning. Novice teachers developing a PBP are empowered to evaluate their progress and improve their skills. Evidence representing the beginning teacher's best work, with reflections, is gathered through a systematic process and is ultimately compiled into a finished product and submitted for licensure review. Because final products are usually limited in size and content, beginning teachers select the evidence that provides the most comprehensive picture possible.

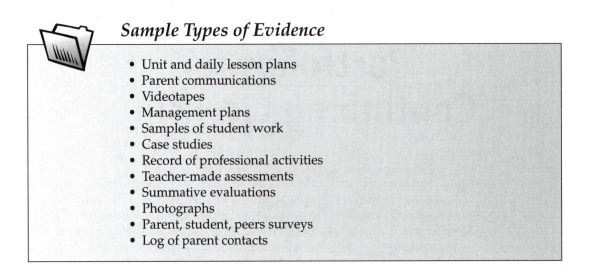

Sample Types of Evidence

- Unit and daily lesson plans
- Parent communications
- Videotapes
- Management plans
- Samples of student work
- Case studies
- Record of professional activities
- Teacher-made assessments
- Summative evaluations
- Photographs
- Parent, student, peers surveys
- Log of parent contacts

As discussed earlier in Chapters 2 and 3, the standards upon which beginning teachers frequently demonstrate their teaching competence are the INTASC standards (see Figure 6–1). The audience for the licensing portfolio is the school system's licensure officer or board or the State Licensing Board assessors. Regardless of who handles licensing, beginning teachers develop the portfolio based on standards in order to secure a continuing license.

ORGANIZATION OF BEGINNING TEACHER PORTFOLIOS

Beginning teacher portfolios are organized around a coordinated set of evidence as prescribed by the employing system and/or state. The evidence may be presented standard by standard. The organization may be presented by areas of teaching such as management, curriculum, instruction, and assessment (see accompanying box). Various activities may be the organizing framework for the portfolio. An example of an activity is

> Create a parent survey that gathers information about how parents perceive your effectiveness as their children's teacher. Randomly choose five parents to complete the survey. Summarize the survey findings. (Figures 6-2 and 6-3 present sample surveys.)

1. **Content Pedagogy**   The teacher understands the central concepts, tools of inquiry, and structures of the discipline he or she teaches and can create learning experiences that make aspects of subject matter meaningful to students.
2. **Student Development**   The teacher understands how children learn and develop, and can provide opportunities that support a child's intellectual, social, and personal growth.
3. **Diverse Learners**   The teacher understands how children differ in their approaches to learning and creates instructional opportunities that are adapted to diverse learners.
4. **Multiple Instructional Strategies**   The teacher understands and uses a variety of instructional strategies to encourage student development of critical thinking, problem solving, and performance skills.
5. **Motivation and Management**   The teacher uses an understanding of individual and group motivation and behavior to create a learning environment that encourages positive social interaction, active engagement in learning, and self-motivation.
6. **Communication and Technology**   The teacher uses knowledge of effective verbal, nonverbal, and media communication techniques to foster active inquiry, collaboration, and supportive interaction in the classroom.
7. **Planning**   The teacher plans instruction based upon knowledge of subject matter, students, the community, and curriculum goals.
8. **Assessment**   The teacher understands and uses formal and informal assessment strategies to evaluate and ensure the continuous intellectual, social, and physical development of the learner.
9. **Reflective Practice: Professional Growth**   The teacher is a reflective practitioner who continually evaluates the efforts of his or her choices and actions on others (students, parents, and other professionals in the learning community) and who actively seeks out opportunities to grow professionally.
10. **School and Community Involvement**   The teacher fosters relationships with school colleagues, parents, and agencies in the larger community to support students' learning and well-

FIGURE 6–1   INTASC Standards

Sample by Area of Organization

- Demonstrating content knowledge and ability to teach
- Classroom management and its environment
- Professional responsibility
- Measurement of student learning

In both of the last two organizational structures, the standards and their specific indicators are identified in the area or activity.

Reflection is the keystone of the performance-based product. It is critical to the novice teacher's development. Through reflection the teacher begins the ongoing process of blending the art and science of effective teaching

The Portfolio Machine

© Thomson 2000

practice. Reflections require thoughtful and careful reporting and analysis of teaching practice, philosophy, and experience. Understanding why an activity or practice was productive or nonproductive in the classroom is a key element in the progression from novice teacher toward master teacher (Dietz, 1995; Sparks, 1997).

The reflections are also vital to the person or persons with the responsibility of judging whether teachers have met the required level of performance for each standard or activity. The reflections allow teachers to learn from their experiences and determine where they have been and where they want to go next.

Parent/Guardian Survey

Teacher's Name: _____

Thank you for your help. The information from this survey will be invaluable to your child's teacher. Please check the following items that describe your experience with the teacher. No individual parents will be identified with these survey forms.

Have you asked for:

	Yes	No
1. An overview of class content and goals?	_____	_____
2. A description of your child's progress?	_____	_____
3. Ideas for home support of learning?	_____	_____

Has the teacher provided you with:

	Yes	No
4. An overview of class content and goals?	_____	_____
5. A description of your child's progress?	_____	_____
6. Ideas for home support of learning?	_____	_____

Circle the number that best describes your opinion.

	Yes				No	Don't Know
7. Did your child seem to know what was expected of him or her in this class?	5	4	3	2	1	0
8. Did the classroom work seem to be the right challenge, not too hard or too easy?	5	4	3	2	1	0
9. Were you satisfied with your child's overall classroom experience as provided by this teacher?	5	4	3	2	1	0

Additional comments:

_____

_____

_____

_____

Please add any additional comments on the back of this form.

FIGURE 6–2 Sample

Parent/Guardian Survey

NAME: _____

RELATIONSHIP TO CHILD: _____

NOTE TO PARENT: Please complete and place this survey in the envelope provided.

	strongly disagree				strongly agree
1. My child is treated fairly by this teacher. Comments:	1	2	3	4	5
2. I know the expectations this teacher has for my child. Comments:	1	2	3	4	5
3. My child likes to attend this teacher's class. Comments:	1	2	3	4	5

4. My child's teacher has kept me informed about my child's progress.
    Comments:

5. My child's teacher keeps me informed through:

Please check all that apply:
_____ phone calls _____ progress reports _____ home visits
_____ letter or memo _____ school conferences _____ other [please specify]

6. My child's teacher contacts me:
Please check only one:
_____ daily   _____ once a week   _____ once a month   _____ never
                         _____ several times   _____ several times a month
                                 each week   _____ as often as needed

7. Describe any changes in your child's attitude toward learning or toward school that you can credit to this teacher.

8. Do you feel that your child is learning in this teacher's classroom? Why or why not?

Please add any additional comments on the back of this form.

FIGURE 6–3 Sample

> **Note:** Review Chapter 3 to refresh your memory on the purpose and construction of reflections.

REFLECTIONS

The reflections included in a performance-based product developed by a beginning teacher focus not only on the activity or area required by the school system or state, but also on the connection between the evidence and the established standards. The reflection helps the beginning teacher put evidence into perspective for the assessors by explaining how the evidence addresses standards through the activity or area. In the case of the INTASC standards, as for most standards, the indicators for each standard are important and must be addressed in the reflection. The following examples show reflections that address standards and indicators.

Sample #1 from a Performance-Based Portfolio

Introduction   Nancy Lilley,* a non-Hispanic white was a first semester senior during her field experience in a rural, low socioeconomic school. Her class, seventh-grade physical science, was composed of students identified as slow learners. Nancy has been present in these students' classroom one day a week for the past month. She had observed the students and provided them one-on-one assistance during her previous days.

Describe   *I taught a lesson on March 30th at 9:30 a.m. that met five of the INTASC standards. The lesson met Standard 1, content knowledge, because I displayed an understanding of the content and effectively transferred that information to the students. It met Standard 2, student development, because I provided for students' various learning styles by using manipulatives, writing exercises, and oral communication. Because of the group's diversity, I provided a variety of experiences, meeting Standard 3, diverse learners. The lesson met Standard 4, multiple teaching strategies, because I used strategies to encourage thinking on different levels, by expecting my students to make connections while stating the obvious. Lastly, I incorporated Standard 5, management and motivation, because I was aware of the important social interaction with this class and used it to create a more positive environment for learning.*

The class was seventh-grade boys and girls, the majority of which were African-American males. Most were repeating the grade and had barely passed the sixth-grade competency test. The class was a lively group and not well disciplined, but I took that into consideration when planning the format I used to teach the lesson.

The lesson focused on simple machines. I began by having the students write a few notes about what they knew about simple machines. Then we brainstormed together about things we see everyday that might be simple machines. Everyone was involved

*Not her real name.

in the discussion. Next I spent 15 minutes describing each of the six simple machines and demonstrating with models I had brought with me. The students were able to watch, to reflect, and then work with the models. We discussed as a large group, worked in small groups which I supervised, and reflected individually about what we saw, touched, and wrote. In addition, I encouraged vocabulary building and note taking with a handout we completed together. During the remaining time, the students worked on hidden word puzzles I created for the lesson.

Analysis   *I used the textbook as the lesson's foundation, but I constructed my own teaching props. There was a great deal of interest because of the immediacy of the subject material. The lesson was the most successful I had taught these students (it was my third). My students were even able to reduce some complicated machines in the world around them to simple terms. Science helped them explain their world. It showed them that science is useful and it is valuable because it was not clear enough to be useful as a reinforcement tool. I had to do more explaining than I planned or wanted to do. The class was not quiet, but for the most part the students all stayed on task. The lesson probably included a little more information than could be efficiently mastered in one class period. The introduction of simple machines alone, without definitions and equations, would have been enough. All in all, the lesson was a positive experience for my students and for me.*

Future Impact   *This teaching episode showed me the value of making academic information relevant and real. For a socially active class like this one, a lesson like this that lent itself to group interactions was positive. I was well prepared and the students were interested, which meant maintaining discipline was easier. It showed me that it is necessary to acknowledge where these students are and what they are interested in. The lesson reinforced the importance of preparation, appropriate teaching strategies, and my students' needs.*

Author's Reaction

Nancy Lilley wrote an informative reflection for a beginning teacher. Her analysis is consistent with concerns of beginning teachers. A strength of the reflection was the linking of the INTASC standards to her teaching experience. An area to improve is the Future Impact section. It could have more detail and correlation with issues discussed in the description and analysis sections. It is important for a teacher to be focused when writing reflections that correlate with standards.

Sample #2 from a Performance-Based Portfolio

Introduction   Jack Morino* is a second-year teacher in a small city. He teaches a fourth-grade elementary class of children from low and middle income homes. The pieces of evidence for this reflection are two floor plans of the classroom, be-

*Not his real name.

fore and after, and the accompanying seating charts. As this sample demonstrates, some PBP reflections may focus on one or more pieces of evidence.

Reflection   *INTASC Standards met by this evidence*

#2. Student Development

#5. Motivation

Much time is spent moving about the classroom, handing things in, going to centers, picking up corrected work, and working on projects and activities. I have set up my classroom so students can get to these places more efficiently without wasting time or steps. I have analyzed my classroom environment and made adjustments such as moving mailboxes to the front of the room from the rear, thus saving time and steps. Desks are arranged in groups so that all can see the front board. At times I place the morning assignments and activities on the front board giving students some choices of what order to complete them. This gives the students choice and helps them manage their time. It also helps them assume responsibility for their own work completion. Examples of classroom arrangements and board assignments can be seen on my video at time mark 00:09.

Students like having the classroom set up to better meet their needs. I listen to students' concerns and try to physically arrange the room to make them comfortable. I have found, if they are too crowded they are not able to concentrate.

I have learned that I have more time to teach and have students engaged in activities if I cut down on the time it takes to do little things like hand out papers and move around the room. This, and my students' suggestions, are what caused me to analyze my room arrangement and my paper procedures.

ASSESSMENT

The assessment of performance-based products involves scoring rubrics to evaluate each activity or area. In education assessment a *rubric* is defined as a scoring guide that indicates the criteria to be used and several levels of performance (Glatthorn, 1998). The most frequently used types of rubric are the holistic and analytical. The *holistic rubric* usually has competency labels associated with them. The following box is an example of a rubric used to assess planning for instruction. It contains three competency labels: skillful, promising, and ineffective; only one score is given for the entire product. That is why it is called a holistic rubric. The *analytical rubric* uses the same set of competency labels for each different category. The rubric is applied across different categories, such as instruction, motivation, and professional growth, and a rating is given for each individual category (Linn & Gronlund, 2000). The analytical rubric is more useful for providing diagnostic feedback because it assesses individual categories, enabling teachers to focus on the specific areas that received high or low ratings. Holistic rubrics, however, tend to be the type used to assess performance-based products in the licensure process. This is because the purpose of the licensure process is to make a yes-or-no decision about whether to issue a license to practice. It is summative in nature and, as such, does not demand specific feedback or ratings by categories.

Planning for Instruction (Rubric Examples)

The Skillful Teacher's planned instructional strategies are designed to regularly engage students and encourage critical thought. This teacher often makes connections between content being presented, the larger unit of study, or the students' daily lives. Materials/manipulatives are used to complement the learning.

The Promising Teacher's planned instructional strategies do not always engage students, alternately boring or frustrating them. The teacher does not always make connections between the lesson, or the rest of the unit, or the students' daily realities. Materials/manipulatives are sometimes used to complement learning.

The Ineffective Teacher relies solely on lecture, worksheets, or workbooks, rarely planning to engage or challenge the students. This teacher does not make connections between lessons, the greater unit of study, or the students' daily lives. Materials are frequently outdated, inappropriate, or not used at all. (From Teach For America's PAI document, 1996)

STATE PERFORMANCE–BASED ASSESSMENT SYSTEMS

Several states are considering or have developed performance-based processes for awarding continuing licenses to beginning teachers. Georgia, Florida, Oregon, Washington, New York, Connecticut, and North Carolina are in various stages of development. Each state has approached the process from a different perspective. Connecticut is generating performance-based guidelines for each discipline and is using the various learned society standards, such as those from the National Council of Teachers of Mathematics, to guide the product and assessment. On the other hand, North Carolina has developed the same PBP process for all teaching areas, employing the INTASC standards.

PBP ORGANIZATION

One organizational option for a performance-based portfolio is to divide it into five areas with each area addressing one or more of the INTASC standards. The five possible areas could be (1) content knowledge and how to teach it;

(2) learners and their unique needs; (3) classroom climate; (4) the school community link; and (5) evaluation of self as a professional. Specific components would be required for each area. For example, consider the area of classroom climate, which would address INTASC Standard 5. The required components for this area would be

- a classroom management plan
- comparison of discipline occurrences at beginning and end of year
- video to support this area
- contact with parents (e.g., a discipline log)
- reflection

Developers would also include additional evidence to document this area and the related INTASC standard. Figure 6-4 is an outline of a classroom management plan.

A management plan is a must for any teacher who wishes to have a classroom that runs smoothly. It is an individual set of procedures and guidelines that reflect what a teacher believes about interacting with young people. The management plan must be developed within the policies and procedure already established by a school system and/or an individual school. This outline is a guide to assist teachers in developing a management plan.

I. **Identify the classroom rules.**
    Remember to get student input and to include the rule, "Follow all school rules."

II. **Identify consequences for breaking or following the rules.**
    The consequences may be different for each rule, or they may be an accumulation of rule violations or successes.

III. **Develop lesson plans to teach the rules and consequences.**
    The most important concept a teacher will teach all year is appropriate behavior in the classroom so it can operate in an efficient and effective manner. Remember that students come from different cultures and backgrounds; thus, the class must discuss some words, phrases, and behaviors to come to a common understanding. This part of your plan should include parent/guardian notification.

IV. **Decide how you will assess whether or not students understand the rules and consequences.**
    This and the teaching of the rules, consequences, and procedures is an ongoing effort. Update and review with the students on a regular basis.

V. **Establish the rules and consequences in the classroom.**
    Remember what students want most from their teacher is to be treated fairly and with consistency.

FIGURE 6-4   Outline of Classroom Management Plan

Another organizational example using the INTASC standards is to begin by dividing the portfolio into 10 standards. Then place pieces of evidence/artifacts into each standard and write a reflection on each artifact or on the standard as a whole. Some pieces of evidence would have a *value-added effect;* that is, they would apply to more than one standard. An excellent example of a value-added artifact is a contiguous set of lessons. Those lessons could be evidence to support INTASC standards 1, 2, 4, 6, 7, and/or 8. At the end of this portfolio, include a reflection on the evidence and product as a whole.

INTRODUCTORY INFORMATION TO THE PBP

No matter what organizational pattern the product takes, some information must be gathered for placement at the beginning of the performance-based portfolio:

1. A biographical data sheet, including information about beginning teachers and the college or university from which they graduated.
2. Demographic data regarding the school setting and the particular demographics of the beginning teacher's classroom (see Figure 6-5).
3. A signature sheet with the signatures of the beginning teacher, mentor, and principal. This sheet is designed to verify that the product has been completed by the teacher who is submitting the product.
4. A checklist to assist beginning teachers in their organization of the product (see Figure 6-6).

Following these information sheets are areas and/or standards with the evidence to support them.

Appendix B provides a sample of how North Carolina is implementing performance-based products, using the INTASC standards for all beginning teachers. It has been chosen for inclusion because it appears to be the most developed, it is applicable to all disciplines, it is highly reliable, and it is being implemented statewide (Jaeger & Wrightman, 1999).

As mentioned previously, Connecticut is also instituting the use of performance-based products for beginning teachers. Its process is discipline specific and as the discipline guidelines are developed, they are being implemented statewide.

The state of Washington has been involved in developing a performance-based portfolio process for many years. It has been implemented in Seattle but is not yet statewide.

Candidate Name: _____ Candidate ID# _____ Soc. Sec. # _____
School: _____ District: _____
Grade(s): _____ Subject(s): _____

Pease use a **BLACK PEN** and **CIRCLE** or **PRINT** your responses in the space provided. Unless otherwise indicated check only one response for each question. Please respond to all questions.

1. Which of the following best describes the **LEVEL** of the class being observed?

   a. Pre-Kindergarten–Grade 2
   b. Grades 3–5
   c. Grades 6–8
   d. Grades 9–12
   e. More than one of the levels above
      (please specify) _____

2. Which of the following best describes the **CONTENT** of the Class being observed?

   a. Business
   b. Computer science
   c. English as a second language
   d. Foreign language
   e. Health/physical education
   f. Home economics
   g. Language arts/communications
   h. Mathematics
   i. Physical/biological/chemical sciences
   j. Social sciences
   k. Special education
   l. Visual arts/ music/theater/dance
   m. Vocational education
   n. Other (please specify) _____

3. Which of the following best describes the areas from which Your students come? (Check **ALL** that apply.)

   a. Low income, urban
   b. Middle or upper income, urban
   c. Low income, suburban
   d. Middle or upper income, suburban
   e. Low income, small town (not suburban)
   f. Middle or upper income, small town
      (not suburban)
   g. Low income, rural
   h. Middle or upper income, rural

4. [   ] What is the **TOTAL NUMBER** of students enrolled in the class to be observed?

5. [   ] a. What is the number of **MALE** students?
        b. What is the number of **FEMALE** Students?

6. [   ] What is the **AGE** range for all of the students in the class?

7. What is the estimated number of students identified in each **RACIAL/ETHNIC GROUP?**

   [   ] a. African American or Black
   [   ] b. Asian American/Asian (Ex.: Japanese, Chinese, Korean)
   [   ] c. Pacific Island American/Pacific Islander
   [   ] d. Mexican, Mexican American, or Chicano
   [   ] e. Other Hispanic, Latino, or Latin American
   [   ] f. Native American, American Indian, or Alaskan Native
   [   ] g. White
   [   ] h. Other (please specify)

8. What is the estimated number of students in each of the following **LANGUAGE** categories?

   [   ] a. English language proficient
   [   ] b. Limited English language proficient

9. Approximately what **PERCENTAGE** of your class can be categorized as the following?

   (Percentage)
   [   ] a. Above-average or advanced skill level
   [   ] b. Average or intermediate skill level
   [   ] c. Below-average skill level
   100% Total

10. Approximately how many students in this class have been identified as having **EXCEPTIONALITIES?**

   [   ] a. Blind or visually impaired
   [   ] b. Deaf or hearing impaired
   [   ] c. Developmentally disabled
   [   ] d. Emotionally or behaviorally disabled
   [   ] e. Gifted
   [   ] f. Learning disabled
   [   ] g. Physically disabled
   [   ] h. Other (please specify)

Adapted from Praxis III, Educational Testing Service

FIGURE 6–5 Sample Class Profile

Checklist

Please complete this checklist to ensure that you have included everything necessary for an assessor to accurately evaluate your Performance-Based Product. **Be sure that all information is contained in your notebook, including your video.**

_____ **Biographical Data Sheet**
_____ **Signature Sheet**
_____ **Class Profile**
_____ **Videotape (no longer than 30 minutes total)**

Category One - Planning and Instruction
_____ Unit plans and goals
_____ Five contiguous lesson plans
_____ Related student work and test/assessment data
_____ Student achievement log
_____ Evidence/artifacts
_____ Video
_____ Video information sheet
_____ Reflection

Category Two - School and Community
_____ Professional contribution log
_____ Contact log
_____ Parent survey(s) and summary
_____ Evidence/artifacts
_____ Reflection

Category Three - Management and Motivation
_____ Classroom management plan
_____ Comparison of discipline rates
_____ Evidence/artifacts
_____ Video
_____ Video information sheet
_____ Reflection

Category Four - Understanding the Learner
_____ Case Studies
_____ Related student work and test/assessment data
_____ Evidence/artifacts
_____ Video
_____ Video information sheet
_____ Reflection

Category Five - Professional Growth
_____ Beginning Teacher Individual Growth Plan (for all years)
_____ Self-administered interview for year 1
_____ Self-administered interview for year 2
_____ Self-administered interview for year 3 (if applicable)
_____ Summative evaluation for year 1
_____ Summative evaluation for year 2
_____ Summative evaluation for year 3 (if applicable)
_____ Reflection

FIGURE 6–6 Sample PBP Checklist

CLOSING THOUGHTS

There is a difference between a portfolio and a product. This chapter has described, and provided examples for, a product. The prescribed collection of evidences which identifies a product is usually based upon what a school system or state has mandated. The product is assessed against an approved or adopted set of standards. This chapter has focused primarily upon the INTASC standards.

The importance of reflections can not be over emphasized, because reflections are evidence of the depth of the teacher's knowledge and understanding. Performance-based products are being introduced in several states as an assessment process for beginning teachers. It is a way for teachers to be more accountable for their own evaluations and professional growth.

REFERENCES

Dietz, M. (1995). Using portfolios for a framework for professional development. *Journal of Staff Development, 16*(2), 40–43.

Glatthorn, A. A. (1998). *Performance assessment and standards based curricula: The assessment cycle.* Thousand Oaks, CA: Corwin Publishing.

Jaeger, R. M., & Wrightman, L. F. (1999). Analysis of the reliability of and degree of adverse impact resulting from use of the 1997–1998 pilot test version of the North Carolina Performance Based Teacher Licensure System: preliminary report. North Carolina contract #0800008119.

_____ (2000). *Performance based licensure handbook.* Raleigh, NC: Department of Public Instruction.

_____ (1996). Performance Assessment Instrument. New York: Teach For America.

Linn, R. L., & Gronlund, N. E. (2000). *Measurement and assessment in teaching,* 8th ed. Upper Saddle River, NJ: Merrill-PrenticeHall, pp. 276–282.

Sparks, D. (1997). An interview with Linda Darling-Hammond. *Journal of Staff Development, 18*(1), 34–36.

Wolf, K. (1991). The schoolteacher's portfolio: Issues in design, implementation, and evaluation. *Phi Delta Kappan, 3,* 129–136.

CHAPTER 7

Portfolios for Alternative Evaluation

Each year teachers are evaluated by their principals. In most cases, there is a preconference, an observation by the principal, and a post-conference. During the observation, some set of approved criteria is used, and during the post-conference the principal reports both strengths and weaknesses to the teacher. Often praise and suggestions for improvement are given to the teacher during the post-conference. The active participant in this process is the principal who observes a teacher interacting with students and makes a judgment about his/her ability to teach effectively. The teacher usually assumes a reactionary role in the post-conference—listening and responding. Evaluations performed in this matter are done "to the teachers" not "with the teachers," because teachers have no voice in the development of the evaluation. They can only react to what is written (Glatthorn, 1996).

The use of teaching portfolios as an alternative form of teacher evaluation is becoming an acceptable method in school districts across the nation (Wolf, Lichtenstein, & Stevenson, 1997). Professionals recognize the complexity of teaching. The traditional teacher observation tools used for evaluation do not capture the 3,000 daily decisions made by teachers (Danielson, 1996). Portfolios as an alternative method allow teachers to have an active voice in their evaluation and use the results as a professional development tool. The process of developing a portfolio empowers teachers by involving them in their own evaluation. This can result in teachers having a sense of control as they use their portfolios to gain a new perspective on their teaching, to promote self-assessment and reflection, to investigate effective practices, and to enhance student learning and their own professional growth (Hunter, 1998). Specific information on preparing a portfolio is presented in Chapter 2.

For the most part, teachers who develop portfolios at this stage in their career do it for their own professional growth. Portfolios created as an alternative to traditional teacher evaluation have two distinct purposes: (1) for teachers to show competence and (2) for teachers to grow professionally. The audience is the principal or immediate supervisor, such as a department chairperson. The opportunity to develop a portfolio as a continuing teacher is reserved for the tenured teacher.

Teachers and administrators choose to implement professional portfolios for several reasons:

1. Portfolios are an alternative to traditional forms of assessment, allowing teachers more of a voice in their evaluation. Some teachers develop portfolios in addition to traditional methods, which can also be a positive experience for teachers because it blends several types of data about their teaching.
2. Teachers become more reflective about their practice as they develop a portfolio because the process of development requires teachers to contemplate their own abilities.
3. A collaborative relationship can be developed between the teacher and administrator.
4. This type of portfolio development can be a precursor to developing a national board portfolio. (Hunter, 1998)

Another reason teachers should develop a portfolio is to provide documentation about their professional life. Components of the portfolio can also be used to apply for teaching awards or leadership positions.

ORGANIZATION

Teaching portfolios developed by continuing teachers can have many different looks. This chapter presents two suggested frameworks for teachers and a different framework for other educators developing a professional portfolio for evaluation purposes. The first two frameworks for teachers are (1) by categories of teaching skills and abilities, and (2) by categories of professional goals. A framework for other educators is presented using categories of job responsibilities. Another option presented is a framework building on the work of Charlotte Danielson (1996) and the domains of PRAXIS III. Educators looking for cutting-edge options may choose to review Chapter 9, which discusses electronic portfolios. Any of the frameworks presented in this chapter can by used in an electronic design. Logistics for design in this chapter focus on the time line teachers use to develop portfolios. Options are for portfolios to be done (or redone) each year by teachers or developed using a "cycle" over several years. Continuous teachers can develop product, process, or showcase portfolios; showcase and product portfolios, respectively, are most popular for evaluation purposes.

Option for Organization: Teaching Skills and Abilities

A portfolio developed by teaching skills and abilities has as its categories different areas of teaching and related activities (nonteaching duties such as committee work). The first four categories of the first framework, described in the following section, are related to a district's evaluation instrument categories. One would find these areas on most teacher evaluation instruments. The last category, other school involvement, relates to a separate criterion on many district evaluation instruments—nonteaching duties such as committee involvement, leadership opportunities, and other types of service to the school and district. The advantage of this design is that the categories give teachers a specific plan to follow, especially if it correlates to an evaluation instrument used by their principals.

Framework One: District Evaluation Instrument Criteria by Categories

1. Content, teaching methods, and strategies—*content of units and lessons taught, and teaching and learning strategies*
2. Class environment—*organization and structure of the classroom*
3. Preparation and organization—*planning instruction*
4. Student evaluation—*student assessment*
5. Other school involvement—*other responsibilities carried out by a teacher*

In a portfolio divided by Framework One domains, you would place evidence in each of the categories to show competence in these areas. If you want to create a showcase portfolio using this design, include best work related to all of the categories.

Framework Two: A Two-Domain Model

Another framework to show teaching skills and abilities has fewer categories, which might make it attractive to some developers.

This option allows teachers to demonstrate their knowledge, abilities, and dispositions using a two-domain design. Think about the two main responsibilities of a teacher: teaching and classroom management. This design highlights these areas. Category one is teaching and assessing students, which is broad enough to include all elements related to teaching. The second category is classroom climate, which includes management, motivation, and communication. These categories also correlate with propositions of the National Board for Professional Teaching Standards (NBPTS).

The advantage of this design is its simplicity. Since many teaching tasks are interrelated, the broadness of category one allows teachers to include a variety of overlapping evidence. Under category two, teachers specifically document their efforts toward classroom management and student motivation. Teachers could develop showcase or product portfolios using this design.

Framework Two Example

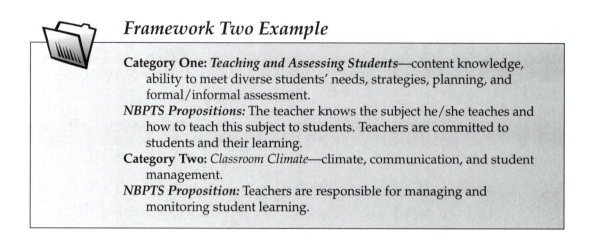

Category One: *Teaching and Assessing Students*—content knowledge, ability to meet diverse students' needs, strategies, planning, and formal/informal assessment.

NBPTS Propositions: The teacher knows the subject he/she teaches and how to teach this subject to students. Teachers are committed to students and their learning.

Category Two: *Classroom Climate*—climate, communication, and student management.

NBPTS Proposition: Teachers are responsible for managing and monitoring student learning.

Framework Three: A Different Kind of Educator

Some teachers or personnel who work in schools don't have traditional teaching responsibilities. Librarians, teacher assistants, and counselors, to name a few, interact with students in a different way than classroom teachers. Thus, traditional organizational formats that outline classroom teaching skills and abilities do not match the job responsibilities of certain school personnel. The process of organizing the portfolio would be the same for these professionals as those set out for teachers outlined earlier in this chapter. A format for these related positions follows.

Category One: Job Responsibilities—*specific responsibilities, as listed in district or state guidelines.*

Category Two: Professional Development—*professional goals set by the educator.*

Option for Organization: Professional Goals as a Framework

Each year teachers, schools, and districts set goals for themselves. Many teachers often create an annual professional development plan in which they identify one to three goals. Often teachers reflect school or district initiatives within their plan. Portfolios are then developed based on the professional goals. Professional goals can be a category within a portfolio, or an entire portfolio can be organized around professional goals. The purpose of a professional goal portfolio is to promote self-learning and continue systematic reflection and growth as professional teachers, no matter how long they have taught. Portfolios created using this framework would follow product portfolio guidelines (see Chapter 2) with developers including evidence that demonstrates they met every professional goal:

1. List professional goal.
2. Outline the goal, identifying how it will be met.
3. Include evidence that shows how each goal is met.
4. Write a reflection on the obtained goal.

Option for Organization: Charlotte Danielson's Framework for Teaching

In this text we have presented several types of national frameworks that are comparable to developing a portfolio. For example, Chapter 6 outlines using the INTASC standards as a framework, and in Chapter 8 the national board framework is presented. Charlotte Danielson's work using the *PRAXIS III: Classroom Performance Assessment* framework philosophically fits with beliefs about practicing teachers' performance in the classroom; thus, this framework can be used as an alternative evaluation tool. PRAXIS III is the final stage developed by the Educational Testing Service for licensure. Some states have adopted this model for licensure while other states use the INTASC standards. In this chapter, we will briefly show how Danielson's model can be a framework for any teacher. For more information on her work or on this framework, refer to her book *Enhancing Professional Practice: A Framework for Teaching* (1996). Danielson's framework is built on four domains:

1. Planning and Preparation
   • Demonstrating Knowledge of Content and Pedagogy
   • Demonstrating Knowledge of Students
   • Selecting Instructional Goals
   • Demonstrating Knowledge of Resources
   • Designing Coherent Instruction
   • Assessing Student Learning
2. The Classroom Environment
   • Creating an Environment of Respect and Rapport
   • Establishing a Culture for Learning
   • Managing Classroom Procedures
   • Managing Student Behavior
   • Organizing Physical Space
3. Instruction
   • Communicating Clearly and Accurately
   • Using Questioning and Discussion Techniques
   • Engaging Students in Learning
   • Providing Feedback to Students
   • Demonstrating Flexibility and Responsiveness

4. Professional Relationships
   - Reflecting on Teaching
   - Maintaining Accurate Records
   - Communicating with Families
   - Contributing to the School and District
   - Growing and Developing Professionally
   - Showing Professionalism (Danielson, 1996)

The advantage of this framework is its universal appeal: It is generic and can be applied across all disciplines. The disadvantage is that it was developed for beginning teachers.

The teacher interested in using this framework would develop a product portfolio much like the INTASC model presented earlier in this text. Other teachers who would like more flexibility may use the four domains as their organizing framework and develop their own quality evidence around each domain.

ORGANIZATIONAL CONSIDERATIONS FOR ALL FRAMEWORKS

Reflections

As we have noted previously, reflection is an essential component of portfolio development. Portfolios for continuing teachers also must contain reflections. For each teaching category, focus your reflections on why you are an effective teacher. Sample reflection questions include: What skills and knowledge am I demonstrating with this evidence? What category am I showing competence in (planning, classroom management, etc.)? What are my strengths as a teacher? (See the sample reflection later in this chapter.)

Reflections should be written for each of the professional goals. Reflections should have several parts: What is the goal? What were the steps to meeting the goal? Was the goal met? How? What did the teacher learn from this goal? What was changed/implemented as a result of this goal? What are the "next steps" based on this goal?

Logistics: Development Options

Continuing teachers can develop a "new" portfolio each year or update their portfolio on a 2- or 3-year cycle. Using a process portfolio design, a 2- or 3-year cycle is set. The cycle works best for the professional goal category. During the first year, the teacher decides on two or three big goals and works on them over the entire cycle. At the end of the first year, progress toward the goals and, possibly, new goals building on these are reviewed and discussed.

At the end of the cycle, a teacher's goal attainment is evaluated. For the next cycle, new goals are set. Another 2- or 3-year cycle option that combines both purposes is as follows:

Year 1:   Teacher shows competency in teaching areas.

Year 2:   If competency is shown in year 1, professional goals are set during this year. At the end of the year, progress toward (or attainment of) professional goals is discussed. New goals may be set that build on initial ones.

Year 3:   Evidence is collected to show goals. At the end of the 3-year cycle, attainment of goals is evaluated by the teacher, then usually the principal.

The next year, a new cycle begins with new goals.

ASSESSMENT

It is important to note that principals or other administrators may reserve the right to decide who will be required to compile a portfolio. If teachers are deemed competent through traditional evaluation methods, they may be given the opportunity to use an alternative type of evaluation. Those teachers who demonstrate competency in the classroom can receive different feedback than teachers who are working toward minimum competency. Thus, feedback may be more informal and should provide teachers with information to help them grow and reflect on their own abilities. Langer (1995) asserts that collaboration between professionals and vision about what a teacher's professional life should be like are two essential components for successful teaching portfolios.

Conferences

Teachers and administrators should have a collaborative conference to discuss the contents of the portfolio. Prior to the conference, administrators should have an opportunity to review and read the portfolio contents. The portfolio framework and categories should drive the conference discussion. Since the administrator is the primary audience for the portfolio, an evaluation using a rubric, checklist, or anecdotal record format may be used. A formal documenting showing "pass/fail" can be included. More helpful to teachers is a written response outlining strengths, insights, and areas to improve or expand. The written feedback will benefit teachers when selecting their next professional goals.

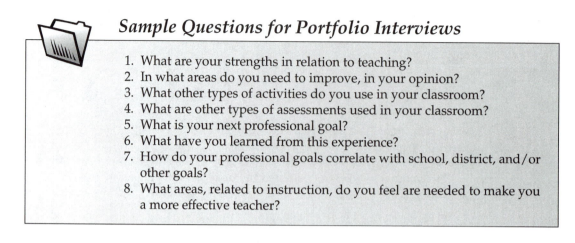

Sample Questions for Portfolio Interviews

1. What are your strengths in relation to teaching?
2. In what areas do you need to improve, in your opinion?
3. What other types of activities do you use in your classroom?
4. What are other types of assessments used in your classroom?
5. What is your next professional goal?
6. What have you learned from this experience?
7. How do your professional goals correlate with school, district, and/or other goals?
8. What areas, related to instruction, do you feel are needed to make you a more effective teacher?

RUBRICS

Another method to judge portfolios is the use of rubrics. A rubric is a scoring guide that gives specific scoring criteria. A rubric may be used to evaluate if a goal is met or not, or if teaching and assessing strategies are at an acceptable standard. While the portfolio is mainly for the teacher, the principal or supervisor will probably need to judge it against the standard. The rubric allows the principal to evaluate the portfolio against the predetermined purpose, thus holding the teacher accountable for the portfolio process. See the sample rubric in Figure 7–1.

So far in this chapter, frameworks, reflections, and assessment have been discussed. Following are examples of portfolios developed by practicing educators using several of the frameworks outlined in this chapter.

SAMPLES OF ALTERNATIVE EVALUATION PORTFOLIOS

Sample #1

Introduction   Carolyn Smith developed her first portfolio in her 29th year of teaching. She teaches third grade in a rural community school. As a tenured teacher, Carolyn chose to develop a showcase portfolio based on the five domains related to teaching. In the first year of a three-year cycle, Carolyn demonstrated her teaching ability through her portfolio. In her classroom, Carolyn uses a unit-based approach based on literature. Her goal is to use a variety of strategies that are hands-on and relevant to students' lives and developmentally appropriate.

Purpose   To demonstrate knowledge, skills, and abilities of teaching; to take charge of her own professional development.

Directions: For this general rubric, a teacher would receive a score for both *Teaching Responsibilities* and *Professional Goals.* This is just an example. Rubrics can be developed by the teacher and administrator; for other sample rubrics, see Danielson (1996).

Teacher: _____ Subjects Taught: _____

Date:

Level	Teaching Responsibilities	Professional Goals
Above Standard	Evidence shows this candidate has the knowledge, skills, and abilities to demonstrate he/she is above standard in relation to teaching responsibilities. Sample Indicators: This teacher uses strategies and skills that are effective and student-centered; assessments that match objectives; and strategies to manage and motivate students to be successful. Critical and other strategies are used with all students. Works well with parents and community.	Evidence shows this candidate has met his/her professional goals in an exemplary way, demonstrated through evidence selected and reflections written. This goal is met and has an impact on thinking skills students' learning in some way.
At Standard	Evidence shows this candidate has the knowledge, skills, and abilities to be at standard in relation to teaching responsibilities. Sample Indicators: Teacher writes and delivers effective lesson plans. A variety of appropriate strategies are used. Classroom is managed appropriately. This teacher does a good job in all areas related to teaching.	The professional goal was met as demonstrated through evidence and reflections written.
Needs Improvement	Evidence shows this candidate may be lacking in some knowledge, skills, or abilities related to teaching responsibilities listed in this column. Area: _____	The professional goal was not met completely. Portions or segments of the goal need to be further developed. Area to Develop: _____
Unacceptable	Evidence shows this candidate is lacking in knowledge, skills, or abilities related to teaching responsibilities listed in this column. This teacher would not have the majority of skills to be effective in the classroom.	The goal was not met.

FIGURE 7–1   Sample Rubric

(continued)

Narrative Feedback		
Strengths		
Areas to Improve		
Future Goals		

_____   _____
Administrator's Signature/Date   Teacher's Signature/Date

Process for Using Scoring Evaluation Criteria:
1. Since portfolios are authentic products, they are used more for self-analysis and reflection. The categories on the rubric are meant to guide discussions about the development of the portfolio for the next school year. Principals and teachers may decide to use one or both categories. A discussion should be held at the preconference stage about the evaluation criteria for the rubric with both parties having an opportunity to discuss their preferences.
2. An area would be selected (at, above, needs improvement, unacceptable).
3. Strengths and Areas to Improve/Future Goals will be filled out for each category.
4. One of the main objectives of this rubric is to promote an *open dialogue* between the teacher and administrator about the portfolio contents.

FIGURE 7–1   (*Concluded*)

Type of portfolio   Showcase using Framework One presented in this chapter

Audience   Principal and herself

Developer   Carolyn Smith, teacher

Assessment   For each piece of evidence, a short description depicted the link between the evidence, domain, and, when appropriate, student learning outcomes. Carolyn wrote a reflection on the entire experience, outlining strengths and futuristic goals. The principal and Carolyn held a conference after the principal reviewed the portfolio. The purpose of the conference was for Carolyn to talk about her portfolio and to clarify any questions or concerns of the principal. The principal gave feedback about each area.

Note   Carolyn Smith presents a very comprehensive portfolio. The amount of evidence may vary for other developers, depending on the subject(s) taught.

Outline of Evidence by Domains Using Framework One—Relationship to District Evaluation Instrument Categories

1. Content, teaching methods, and strategies—content of units and lessons taught, teaching and learning strategies, student learning

   Evidence:
   a. picture of class
   b. year-long planning guide showing units divided by grading period— This provides the overview for the rest of evidence because of its

FIGURE 7–2   Smith Evidence 1e: Students buddy read as one reading strategy in my classroom.

organization and detail. Following it are documents that support the year-long planning guide. This class is literature based (evidence "c-h").

c. morning work—student samples
d. pictures of modeled writing lessons with student work that included all steps in the writing cycle
e. pictures of buddy readers (daily activity)
f. pictures and student work examples of different literature stories read throughout the year
g. pictures showing how teacher assistant is used in class
h. pictures of guest speaker as a follow-up to a literature story
i. science fair pictures
j. field trip brochure
k. graphs showing scientific experiment as a class
l. science labs
m. pictures of various strategies used in class

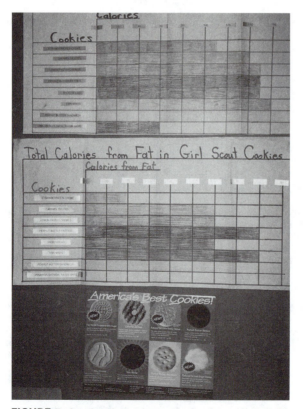

FIGURE 7–3   Smith Evidence 1k: Students do "cookie exploration experiment" in science.

      n. pictures of peer tutors at work
      o. copy of verification log showing students reading 30 minutes a day
2. Class Environment—*organization and structure of the classroom*
      a. pictures of bulletin boards
      b. daily learning calendar for science (copy)
      c. pictures of classroom
      d. behavior and homework charts
      e. motivation homework pass
      f. daily communication letter to parents (for problems)
      g. "Stick" self-discipline program (each day students receive four sticks, taken away if they misbehave; students who keep sticks all day get a small prize
      h. birthday celebration pictures
      i. supplementary reading incentives program
      j. student of the week certificate and bulletin board
      k. description of class service project
      l. parent communication examples (letters, conference sign-up, newsletters)
3. Preparation and organization—*planning instruction*
      a. grade level meeting documentation
      b. student information sheet
      c. copies of lesson plan book for one week
      d. copies of one month's planning guide (planning meetings by grade level)
      e. unit guide
4. Student evaluation—*student assessment*
      a. checklist for writing assignments
      b. weekly reports sent to parents
      c. graphic organizers used by students
      d. traditional test examples
      e. worksheet
      f. differentiated test for special needs learner
      g. sample of grade book
      h. Accelerated Reader report
      i. science lab write-ups
5. Other school involvement—*other responsibilities carried out by a teacher*

      a. Home School Relations Committee pictures
      b. pictures of working with university intern
      c. school service learning project organization
      d. cards and letters expressing thanks for different levels of involvement (attending PTA, helping out someone, etc.)
      e. letter from principal thanking Carolyn for committee involvement
      f. professional organization membership card

FIGURE 7–4   Smith Evidence 5b: Carolyn Smith works with her university intern.

Sample #2

Introduction   Nicole Byrd-Phelps* is a K-12 music teacher in a small, rural district. Each week she teaches general music to all elementary students and band and chorus at a small high school. This is her seventh year of teaching in the same school, where she is tenured. This is her first year developing a portfolio.

Purpose   To demonstrate knowledge, abilities, and disposition as a professional

Type of portfolio   Product using Framework Two presented earlier in this chapter. Each teacher was required to place certain evidence in each domain. Sample evidence could also be added.

Developer   Nicole Byrd-Phelps

Audience   Principal and teacher

Organization   By domains using Framework Two (two categories)

*Contributed by Nicole Byrd-Phelps

Category One   Teaching, Learning, and Assessing Content Knowledge
Required evidence

1. Choose goal and objectives from state curriculum.
2. Create a unit of study using various teaching and learning strategies.
3. Include a videotape of one or more teaching episodes.
4. Present sample student work.
5. Write a reflection.

Nicole's required evidence
 a. *unit focus: Sound for elementary students*
 b. *videotape of class activities during sound unit*
 c. *detailed lesson plans from unit*
 d. *sample work on videotape (sound activities)*
 e. *formal test taken by students*
 f. *reflection on domain one*

Optional evidence for domain one:
 a. *newspaper articles about band and chorus presentations*
 b. *band and chorus concerts programs (many)*
 c. *certificates from band and chorus competitions*
 d. *log of after-school music activities*

Category Two: Classroom Climate
Required evidence

1. classroom rules and consequences
2. list of motivating strategies used in classroom
3. documentation of parent contact
4. discipline log
5. reflection

Nicole's required evidence
 a. *band, chorus, and general music rules and consequences*
 b. *rewards and incentives (tangible and nontangible) for motivating students*
 c. *grading system*
 d. *parent student agreement letter*
 e. *band and chorus handbooks*
 f. *chorus schedule*
 g. *sample parent letters*
 h. *discipline record with consequences*
 i. *parent contact log*

Nicole's Domain One Reflection   *Domain one encompasses teaching, learning, and assessing content knowledge. As teachers, we are responsible for knowing our subject matter and being able to present it in an interesting, motivating fashion. Evidences of such mastery of one's subject area include prepared units of study that include a variety of teaching strategies, a videotape of one teaching episode in a highly motivating manner and example of student work.*

In my school district, it is a goal that teachers continue to grow and enhance their knowledge of their subject areas through professional development activities. Furthermore, in our school's mission statement there is a reference to students being able to experience "the joy of learning" at our school. Therefore, to fulfill this goal and this mission statement, it is important for me as a teacher to constantly add to my extensive knowledge and to keep learning how to present it better.

In order to show my mastery of subject matter, I have included pictures, programs, and newspaper articles, which relate events in which my students or I have participated. Some of the pictures and articles show my students participating in events which reflect their acquisition of musical knowledge and performance skills; whereas I am pictured, discussed, or acknowledged in some of this material to better show my abilities and achievements. Though I did not have to include these items, I thought they would better show just what has been happening in my teaching career with my students since its beginning seven years ago. It is humbling to see the good things that have been accomplished, and I am very thankful for the progress of the music program at the high school and my progress as a teacher.

I have included a list of after-school activities that I have coordinated as the music director at both schools. The list comprises after-school practices, performances, PTA meetings at which students have performed, and individual help sessions. I have also included a unit of study about sound, which is used in general music classes. I feel that it reflects good integration of science and music.

I feel that my mastery of musical subject matter is superior. My evaluations offer proof for this. I enjoy learning more about music, and so, this continued thirst for knowledge will result in my continued acquisition and sharing of new knowledge for my students. The level of my students does not allow me to teach everything I would like. I must do a variety of activities for them to understand one concept, so there is not a lot of time for extra things like music history or theory. Due to our extensive number of performances, at the high school level we spend a lot of time learning and practicing different songs. "Products" win over the "process method" of learning music due to time restraints and limited enrollment reflected in the size of the school (less than 150 in grades 6 through 12).

As I continue to teach, I hope to improve my teaching processes for learning music so students could sight read better, thus learn music quicker. I also intend to add some software programs and other teaching aids into my general music class. These should spur interest and make learning fun. Hopefully, by continuing to upgrade my instructional methods, I will have extremely musically literate students who are excited about communicating the value of their musical experiences in my class to others.

Sample #3

Introduction   Rebecca is an elementary school teacher who set as a professional goal to increase technology.

Purpose   To demonstrate if professional goal is met.

Type of Portfolio   Product using Professional Goal Framework

Organization   By goal(s)

Developer   Teacher

Audience   Principal and teacher

Rebecca's professional goal   To increase technology competency and apply it in the classroom

Evidence

1. certificate of technology workshops attended
2. sample technology products
3. lesson plans that incorporate technology
4. student technology products

Sample #4

Introduction   Tom is a high school health teacher whose district is implementing quality education initiatives. His professional goal reflects a district goal of implementing quality tools in each classroom.

Tom's professional goal   To incorporate quality tools (plus/delta charts, fishbone problem-solving designs) into the classroom

Evidence

1. lesson plans showing quality tools as part of lesson
2. student work using quality tools
3. sample plus/deltas and fish diagrams from whole class discussion
4. changes incorporated in classroom/lessons based on whole class discussions

CLOSING THOUGHTS

Teachers who create portfolios as an alternative evaluation method learn many things about themselves. Over the past four years, we have helped hundreds of teachers develop portfolios. Common responses are: "I like being in charge of myself." "I learned more about my teaching than all of the years I was observed put together." and "I could clearly see my own strengths and weaknesses based on evidence and the reflection process." Finally, "creating a portfolio made me look forward to year 30—I wish I had kept a portfolio since year one, imagine my growth," noted Carolyn Smith, a teacher of 31 years.

The process of creating a portfolio in the 5th, 10th, 20th, or 30th year of teaching can rejuvenate teachers and give them autonomy to help themselves grow professionally—something that is invaluable as a teacher.

REFERENCES

Danielson, C. (1996). *Enhancing professional practice: A framework for teaching.* Alexandria, VA: Association for Supervision and Curriculum Development.

Glatthorn, A. (1996). *The teacher's portfolio: Fostering and documenting professional development.* Rockport, MA: Pro>Active Publications.

Hunter, A. (1998). The power, production, and promise of portfolios for novice and seasoned teachers. In *Professional portfolio models: Applications in education.* Norwood, MA: Christopher-Gorden Publishers.

Langer, G. (1995). Teacher portfolio assessment. *Education Update, 37*(3), 3.

Wolf, K., Lichtenstein, G., & Stevenson, C. (1997). "Portfolios in Teacher Evaluation" (29 pgs.) (Educational Resource Information Center document # ED 409378 Paper Presented at the Annual Meeting of The American Educational Research Association in Chicago, IL, March 24–28, 1997).

CHAPTER 8

Portfolios for Master Teachers

The capstone event for teachers developing a portfolio is the national board certification experience. Teachers who are nationally board certified are considered master teachers. The National Board for Professional Teaching Standards (NBPTS) is an independent, nonprofit, nonpartisan organization. In 1986, the Carnegie Corporation's Task Force on Teaching as a Profession released the report *A Nation Prepared: Teachers for the 21st Century*. This report recommended the establishment of the NBPTS. Based on this action and recommendations in *A Nation Prepared* (follow-up to *A Nation at Risk*), the NBPTS was established in 1987. The mission of NBPTS is to establish high and rigorous standards for what accomplished teachers should know and be able to do and then certify teachers who meet these standards. The thrust of this mission is to improve student learning in American schools by improving teaching through continued reform (NBPTS, 1999).

The NBPTS makes a difference in how district, university, and state department personnel perceive teachers and, equally as essential, how teachers view themselves. Nationally board certified (NBC) teachers must be reflective practitioners who can identify their strengths and weaknesses and show the impact of teaching practices on students' learning (http://www.nbpts.org). Barbara B. Kelley, a physical education teacher in Bangor, Maine, and chair of the NBPTS, states, "These candidates serve as excellent role models for their students by being life-long learners" (Rose, 1999, p. 4). Many unions were hesitant about supporting the NBC process when it began but have come around to endorse the process. Negotiations for support groups and fee reimbursements for applications are prevalent in unions across the country. Teacher unions are beginning to see the NBC process as another mechanism to raise teacher professionalism and salaries (Rose, 1999). Even if unions do not support or discourage the NBC process, teachers should review NBPTS materials and decide for themselves. The process is *voluntary*. All information found by the authors while researching this text indicated positive effects for teachers who completed this process.

THE FOUNDATIONAL BELIEFS OF THE NBPTS

The NBPTS is based on five propositions of accomplished teaching. NBC teachers enhance student learning and demonstrate the high level of knowledge, skills, abilities, and commitments reflected in the five core propositions (NBPTS, 1999).

Proposition One: Teachers are committed to students and their learning.

Major tenets Accomplished teachers:

1. are dedicated to making knowledge accessible to all students.
2. believe all students can learn.
3. treat students equitably, recognizing individual differences and reflecting students' diverse needs in practice.
4. understand how students develop and learn.
5. incorporate cognitive and intelligence theories into practice.
6. are aware of contextual and cultural influences.
7. develop students' cognitive capacity and their respect for learning.
8. Foster students' self-esteem, motivation, character, civic responsibility, and their respect for individual, cultural, religious, and racial differences.

Proposition Two: Teachers know the subjects they teach and how to teach those subjects to students.

Major tenets Accomplished teachers:

1. have a rich understanding of the subject(s) they teach and appreciate how knowledge in their subject is created, linked to other disciplines, and applied to real-world settings.
2. develop the critical and analytical capacities of their students.
3. command specialized knowledge of how to convey and reveal subject matter to students.
4. are aware of the preconceptions and background knowledge that students bring to each subject.
5. are aware of strategies and instructional materials that are appropriate.
6. modify practice according to students' difficulties.
7. create multiple paths to knowledge.
8. teach students how to pose and solve their own problems.

Proposition Three: Teachers are responsible for managing and monitoring student learning.

Major tenets Accomplished teachers:

1. create, enrich, maintain, and alter instructional settings to capture and sustain the interest of their students and to make the most effective use of time.

2. are adept at engaging students and colleagues to assist their teaching.
3. command a range of generic instructional techniques, knowing when to use each one.
4. are aware of ineffectual or damaging practice.
5. know how to engage students.
6. know how to organize instruction so schools' goals are met.
7. are adept at setting norms for social interaction among students and between students and teachers.
8. understand how to motivate students and maintain their interest.
9. can assess the progress of individual students and the whole class.
10. can employ multiple methods for measuring student growth.
11. can clearly explain student performance to parents.

Proposition Four: Teachers think systematically about their practice and learn from experience.

Major tenets   Accomplished teachers:

1. are models of educated persons, exemplifying the virtues they seek to inspire in students—curiosity, tolerance, honesty, fairness, respect for diversity, and appreciation of cultural differences.
2. have the ability to reason and take multiple perspectives to be creative and take risks.
3. can adopt an experimental and problem-solving orientation.
4. draw on their knowledge of human development, subject matter, and instruction and their understanding of students to make principled judgments about their practice.
5. make decisions based on literature and experience.
6. engage in lifelong learning.
7. strive to strengthen their teaching.
8. critically examine their practice.
9. seek to expand their repertoire, deepen their knowledge, sharpen their judgment, and adapt their teaching to new findings, ideas, and theories.

Proposition Five: Teachers are members of learning communities.

Major tenets   Accomplished teachers:

1. contribute to the effectiveness of the school by working collaboratively with other professionals on instructional policy, curriculum development, and staff development.
2. can evaluate school progress and the allocation of school resources in relation to state and local educational objectives.
3. are knowledgeable about specialized school and community resources for students' benefit and can employ resources as needed.

4. work collaboratively and creatively with parents, engaging them productively in the work of the school.

THE STANDARDS

Standards based on the five propositions are developed in more than 30 areas. Teachers wishing to seek national board certification should review all related standards to see which set best correlates with their teaching assignment. There are individual standards for each area of certification. While many sets of NBC standards have similarities, because components of teaching are similar across content and age spans, each individual set of standards is specific for the area of certification. Therefore, careful review of standards is important.

One Set of Standards: Early Childhood/Generalist

I. Knowledge of Young Adolescents—Accomplished generalists draw on their knowledge of early adolescent development and their relationships with students to understand and foster their students' knowledge, skills, interests, aspirations, and values.

II. Knowledge of Subject Matter—Accomplished generalists draw on their knowledge of subject matter to establish goals and to facilitate student learning within and across the disciplines that comprise the middle grades curriculum.

III. Instructional Resources—Accomplished generalists select, adapt, create, and use rich and varied resources.

IV. Learning Environment—Accomplished generalists establish a caring, stimulating, inclusive, and safe community for learning where students take intellectual risks and work independently and collaboratively.

V. Meaningful Learning—Accomplished generalists require students to confront, explore, and understand important and challenging concepts, topics, and issues in purposeful ways.

VI. Multiple Paths to Knowledge—Accomplished generalists use a variety of approaches to help students build knowledge and strengthen understanding.

VII. Social Development—Accomplished generalists foster students' self-awareness, self-esteem, character, civic responsibility, and respect for diverse individuals and groups.

VIII. Assessment—Accomplished generalists employ a variety of assessment methods to obtain useful information about student learning and development and to assist students in reflecting on their own progress.

IX. Reflective Practice—Accomplished generalists regularly analyze, evaluate, and strengthen the effectiveness and quality of their practice.

    X.   Family Partnerships—Accomplished generalists work with families to achieve common goals for the education of their children.

    XI.   Collaboration with Colleagues—Accomplished generalists work with colleagues to improve schools and to advance knowledge and practice in their field. (http://www.nbpts.org)

Similar standards are developed for specific categories. The purpose of the standards is to make the propositions specific to the discipline. When creating a national board portfolio, you should keep those standards and propositions foremost in your mind.

TIME LINE

Teachers apply in the summer for their national board packet and complete the requirements within a five-month period. The "box," containing instructions and materials, arrives in November or December and must be postmarked in April. Candidates must turn in initial verification documentation within a few weeks of receiving the box. Look for this information immediately and return the correct forms. Teachers report they spend about 120 hours compiling their portfolio. Notification of certification status comes approximately 6 months after all parts have been completed. National certification is valid for 10 years (NBPTS, 1998).

What Is Required?

While each certification area requires different activities that correlate specifically to the standards, each ask for the same general requirements:

1. Four or five classroom-based activities with student work samples
2. A videotape that correlates with one or more of the classroom-based activities
3. Work outside the classroom with parents, families, colleagues, and communities
4. Documented accomplishments as a professional
5. Written reflections on each activity

Early Childhood/Generalist Activities

- Introduction to Your Classroom Community—Teachers show how they structure their time, establish rules and routines, and organize space and materials in ways that promote children's social development, mutual respect, and emerging independence. Activity includes a written commentary (reflection) and videotape highlighting student interaction.

- Reflecting on a Teaching and Learning Sequence—Teachers submit a written commentary and supporting artifacts, which show how they nurture children's growth and learning as they explore a theme drawn from social studies and the arts.
- Engaging Children in Science Learning—Teachers present a learning experience that engages children in the investigation of a science concept. Videotape, written detailed explanation of experience, relationship to sequence of activities for learning science concepts, and written commentary are required.
- Examining a Child's Literacy Development—Teachers present ways they foster literacy development in their classroom. They must analyze work samples from one child and discuss how the child's literacy development was supported. Written commentary and child's work samples are required.
- Documented Accomplishments—Teachers document work outside the classroom, with parents, and in the profession. They must highlight their commitments to families and communities and their contributions to the teaching profession. Two summaries are required of their accomplishments, one for families and one for profession.

Requirements for Evidence

Several of the activities for each set of standards require supporting evidence, called *artifacts* in the NBPTS literature. Keep these requirements in mind when compiling evidence:

1. No artifact may be larger than 8.5 by 11 inches.
2. Do not send any three-dimensional artifacts or original artwork— photograph them.
3. Count each photograph as one artifact.
4. Do not submit videotapes (beyond the required one) or audiotapes; transcribe relevant conversations.
5. Do not send class sets of work; a work sample from one child counts as one artifact.
6. Delete the last names of children or any identifying information about their families.
7. Label each artifact with a number placed in the upper right-hand corner. Use this number in the Written Commentary when referring to the artifact. For example: "Artifact #2 is an anecdotal record on my observations of children constructing the city. I noted that they did not understand that the water supply needed to be elevated because of the lack of sufficient natural waterpower. As a result, I elaborated on the concept the following day." (Example from NBPTS web site: http://www.nbpts.org/nbpts/seeking/sample-portflio.html)

NATIONAL BOARD ASSESSMENT CENTER EXERCISES

The second part of national board certification is the assessment center exercises. This written test is based on challenging teacher issues and includes evaluating other teachers' practices and interview and content exams in a teacher's field. Each year, there is a "window," usually during the summer, when this written assessment must be taken. This window is usually between 2 and 4 weeks, depending on the area of certification.

Good Information about the Written Assessment

1. This assessment is taken at Sylvan Assessment Centers (1-800-967-1100) across the country.
2. Specific resources can be taken into the testing area. NBPTS identifies these by certification areas. In some certification areas, candidates are required to read specific books or do certain tasks prior to taking the written assessment.
3. Candidates must reserve a day for their assessment in advance.
4. The center exercises are usually four 90-minute essays, which test knowledge and practical application in standards' area.
5. Candidates can take the written assessment using paper and pencil or complete the exam on the computer. Consider the type of test you will be taking—if it will contain math symbols, paper and pencil might be easier unless you are extremely computer literate.
6. The tests are timed and can contain multiple essay questions related to the discipline.

ASSESSMENT

Teachers are trained to assess the portfolio and assessment center exercises. Professional teachers apply to be assessors and are trained extensively to judge portfolios accurately. Scoring is based on all of the candidate's responses: videotapes, student work samples, written documentary, and center exercises. The key to assessment is meeting the standards. Criteria for assessment are based on the standards. When you are reviewing your portfolio, refer to the standards continually. Each activity and center exercise receives a score that can be banked, if a section is not passed. Teachers may redo any portfolio activity or center exercise and submit them to be rescored.

It is important for candidates to make sure each portfolio activity is complete. When packing the portfolio, put each activity in its separate envelope. These activities are assessed separately. Evaluators will not know your students, school, or other demographics so provide any information that you can, following NBPTS directions (NCAE, 1998).

Scoring Specifics

Assessors use guiding questions and rubrics to assess portfolio activities. Guiding questions reflect the standards. The guiding questions are designed to help assessors focus on the exact nature of the candidate's materials and determine the ways in which those materials reflect the criteria in the directions and in the rubric.

The four-point holistic rubric for each activity contains language that reflects performance. The wording is precise. Four words help define criteria in the rubrics:

- *Convincing* speaks to the specificity of the evidence, connections made to its importance by the teacher, the appropriateness of the reasons for actions and inferences the teacher gives.
- *Consistent* speaks to how the evidence from all sources tends to convey a coherent picture of the teacher's practice.
- *Convincing and significant* focuses on the relevance and importance of the evidence. Does evidence from all sources support the judgment that this is an accomplished practitioner? Is the description precise, specific, and detailed?
- *Plausible* speaks to the believability of the evidence, given the assessor's professional expertise and experience. This is in relation to standards and reasonable expectations (NCAE, 1998).

Sample Portfolio Language Framework

Standards for each entry are reflected throughout the portfolio.

Level 4: clear, consistent, convincing, accurate reflection of what is there
Level 3: clear evidence, not as strongly/clearly articulated, less detailed
Level 2: limited evidence, vague goals
Level 1: little or no evidence or goals, items missing or weak, little or no reflection about students, rationale is missing, weak or unrelated (NCAE, 1998)

Specific Evaluation Criteria

Specific criteria are reflected throughout all activity rubrics. Some examples include:

- Knowledge of students: specific, detailed, individualized
- High expectations for student achievement in the context of the particular class
- Appropriate goals/activities for particular class and students

- Worthwhile goals/activities for particular class and activities
- Insightful/perceptive analysis

Scoring

The scale score has four ordinal points, ranging from low (1) to high (4). In addition, assessors use pluses and minuses to indicate gradations of performance that can't be represented by the scale scores (e.g., 0.75, 1.0, 1.25, 1.75, 2.0, 2.25, etc.) (NBPTS, 1998)

OTHER RELEVANT INFORMATION

1. Applications are available by calling or writing NBPTS at 1-800-22-TEACH; www.nbpts.org; or National Board for Professional Teaching Standards, 26555 Evergreen Road, Suite 400, Southfield, Michigan 48076.
2. The application fee is $2,000. A minimum of $500.00 is due with the application. Applications are usually due in November.
3. Sample portfolios are available for purchase from NBPTS. Before a teacher pays $2,000, it would be helpful to order a sample.
4. Different states have various incentives and financial support for national board certification. For example, North Carolina pays for the fee for a finite number of teachers and gives teachers a 12 percent raise. Mississippi NBC teachers who are employed receive a $3,000 salary supplement and the certification fee is reimbursed. Many other states offer scholarships or partial reimbursements for application fees through grants and other monies. School districts within various states may also award incentives above those provided by state legislatures.
5. Thirty-three to forty percent of candidates are successful on their first try (NCAE, 1998).
6. More than 36 states recognize national board certification for licensure.

TIPS FROM NATIONALLY CERTIFIED TEACHERS

Teachers who have successfully completed the certification process offer this advice:

1. Apply for certification in the *appropriate* area. Reviewing standards for various areas will help a candidate determine in which category to apply for best results.
2. Review general descriptions of activities for each set of standards to help make the decision. If you can't think of an activity that would be appropriate for each standard, then look at a different set of standards.

Many overlap so a candidate should not "make up" or "force" any lessons or student work for any activity.

3. Create a support network. Tell students and administrators. Ask family members for support. Don't take on extra responsibilities during this time.
4. Enlist a colleague to seek certification at the same time you do. He or she will provide the best incentive to finish.
5. Plan some milestones and celebrations during the 5 months.
6. Make a plan and stick with it. First, review units and choose the ones that best fit the activities. Schedule time to work on your activities each week.
7. Plant a video camera in the classroom. Let the students get used to it.
8. Find a proofreader who will be honest. Make sure this person will invest the time needed (6–8 hours) and will give constructive feedback.
9. Once you receive the box of materials, read everything.
10. Keep the box. Activities are packed in it to return for scoring.
11. Fill out the initial paperwork when it arrives. It is due soon.
12. Use a highlighter to outline important instructions.
13. Carry around a pad to jot down ideas and record reflections. Put it by the bed because many times the best ideas come in the middle of the night!
14. Put a box in the classroom to put samples and other evidence in that might be helpful later.
15. Buy Post-it notes to use on planning charts (supplied in portfolio box). If you change your mind, then you can revise the planning idea.
16. Keep portfolios of student work samples—not just the best work but a variety of student work.
17. Keep a loaded camera in the classroom. A disposable camera will work, if it has a flash.
18. Keep a journal. Practice writing reflections before doing portfolio reflections.
19. Keep a phone log of parent communications.
20. Experiment with your video equipment to make sure voices can be heard on the videotape.
21. Label the videotape with date and related entry.
22. Inform the school office and put a sign on your door when you videotape. Remember, the video camera cannot be stopped, so interruptions can hinder a candidate.
23. Get on the contact list for support. Applicants are sent a list of all candidates for that year. Call your colleagues.
24. Read everything and organize it into a three-ring binder.
25. Get student release forms signed and returned immediately. Candy works well as an incentive.

26. Each candidate receives a "number." Print pages of these on crack-and-peel adhesive paper to stick on each page.
27. Set aside an entire day to fill out the forms and package product.
28. Begin early and stick with it.
29. Break down entries. Tackle one at a time. Start with documented accomplishments or activities.
30. Use a lot of self-talk. This is time consuming, but worthwhile.

REFLECTIONS

In the national board process, the reflection is called a *written commentary*. These commentaries tend to be approximately 10 pages. The written commentary contains three types of writing: description, analysis, and reflection. Descriptions should be clear and precise, especially with those entries that have no accompanying videotapes. A candidate must paint a picture for the assessor. The analysis section answers the question *why*. Why are lessons taught in a certain way? How and in what way are things carried out in the classroom? Reflection is the self-analysis section. What did you infer about your practice? In retrospect, what does this entry show about your teaching?

Write clearly and to the point. Candidates should add any comments that will help prove what is shown in the evidence meets the *standards*. Content is important and should parallel with evidence. A good portfolio will have strong evidence and a convincing commentary. Both must relate to the standards (NCAE, 1998).

Follow these recommendations as you develop the written commentary:

1. Word process everything. That makes changes easier.
2. Stick to the page length. Anything over the limit will NOT be read.
3. Set one-inch margins on all sides.
4. Double-space the text.
5. Number the pages.
6. Use 10 or 12 point font; no less than 10 characters per inch.
7. If you use subtitles to break down commentary, these will "count" in the page count (NBPTS, 1998).
8. Review commentary to make sure all questions in directions have been answered.

The written commentary is an important component of the portfolio because it provides documentation and clarification for the evidence. Clear, consistent language will help the assessor understand the intent of the candidate.

SAMPLE PORTFOLIO EXERCISE

An NBC high school mathematics teacher who is certified in adolescence and young adulthood mathematics wrote the NBC reflection in Appendix C. This teacher has spent 15 years in the classroom. She is involved professionally on the district, state, and national level. In addition, she works with the area university as a clinical teacher for undergraduate students and on special projects. She is a master teacher.

NBC Packet Directions for This Reflection

Entry One: Analysis of Student Work: Applications

Accomplished mathematics teachers understand their students and center their classrooms around students. They design lessons considering differing aptitudes, knowledge, interests, and ways of learning. They create situations that encourage students to explore and build upon previous knowledge and understandings, and enable students to recognize the connections among concrete, symbolic, and graphical representations. They create learning experiences in which students analyze a wide range of patterns from all aspects of scientific, technical, and practical work. They use calculators and computers as instructional resources to help students represent and reason about mathematical patterns. They have a broad and deep knowledge of the discipline, of the important mathematical domains, and of the processes of mathematical thinking. They design lessons to engage students in problem solving, mathematical communication, reasoning, and searching for connections. They have a clear understanding of the connections between mathematics and other fields of human endeavor, and connections within the strands of mathematics.

They design their lessons with important mathematical goals and select instructional techniques and activities that allow students to meet these goals. They make effective judgments related to content choice, sequence, emphasis, and instruction that will facilitate student understanding, communication, and reasoning. They identify, assess, adapt, and create instructional resources to enhance student learning.

They design appropriate and varied strategies to assess processes and products of students' mathematical explorations and problem-solving activities, modify lessons based on assessment results, and provide timely and instructive feedback to students. They reflect on what they teach and how they teach, seeking to improve their knowledge and practice.

For the entry teachers must:

1. Select three students who represent different kinds of challenges to them.
2. Submit an assignment or prompt that requires students to explore and/or engages students in making important connections among ideas in mathematics or between mathematics and contexts outside

mathematics to help students better understand the mathematics being studied.

3. Submit the responses of the three students selected to this assignment.
4. Submit a **Written Commentary of no more than 11 pages** that contextualizes, explains, and analyzes this teaching.

The Written Commentary must address:

1. *Instructional Context:* The relevant features of your teaching setting; How the instructional context affects practice. [suggested length—1 page]
2. *Planning:* What are the learning objectives? Where does this assignment fit in the instructional sequence for the unit? What is the rationale for using this particular assignment in light of overall learning goals for the lesson, unit, and year? How was the assignment designed to elicit mathematical reasoning and thinking from students? [suggested length—2 pages]
3. *Analysis of Three Student Responses:* Why was each student chosen? What challenges does the student represent? What does one need to know about each student to understand the attached response? How does each student's work reflect (or not reflect) the learning objectives? How was feedback given to the students? [suggested length—6 pages]
4. *Reflection:* What does each student's work suggest about the teacher's "next steps" in instruction? What would the teacher do differently next time this lesson was taught (prior to, during, or after)? What would be repeated? Why? [suggested length—2 pages] (NBPTS, 1998)

See Appendix C for the sample reflection.

CLOSING THOUGHTS

Teachers take on an inspiring goal when they decide to apply for national board certification. Those who want to be successful in this endeavor should understand and embrace the standards in their area. This time-consuming process is valuable to teachers. Those who have succeeded have found out much about themselves as teachers and are proud to be called a nationally certified teacher, a title held by a small percentage of the teaching profession.

REFERENCES

National Board for Professional Teaching Standards (1999).
http://www.nbpts.org.

National Board for Professional Teaching Standards (1998). *Guide to national board certification.* Southfield, MI: NBPTS.

North Carolina Association of Educators. (1998). NBPTS information session and handouts. Raleigh, NC: NCAE.

Rose, M. (1999). *American teacher, 83,* 6–7, 14. Washington, DC: American Federation of Teachers.

CHAPTER 9

Electronic Portfolios

Written by David Powers, Scott Thomson, and Kermit Buckner

One of the most exciting recent developments in portfolio design has been the emergence of electronic portfolios. Picture for a moment every item in your portfolio collected, organized, and presented electronically. Imagine being able to connect any material in your portfolio instantaneously to any other material by simply clicking a button on the screen. Imagine all of the material in your three-ring binders, file boxes, and accordion files efficiently organized on a single CD-ROM. All of these options are surprisingly easy to do using technologies presently available in most schools.

ELECTRONIC PORTFOLIOS

An electronic portfolio contains essentially the same material that would be placed into a traditional portfolio. These materials, however, are captured, organized, saved, and presented electronically. The electronic portfolio typically contains digital photographs, scanned images, text files, audio, video, and combinations of these formats. The electronic portfolio may be saved to a CD, a large capacity disk (such as Zip disks or Jaz disks), and/or the hard drive of your computer. Items placed into an electronic portfolio may be linked to other items in the portfolio or to windows that open to provide reflection, interpretation, or additional detail. Electronic portfolios may be created in a variety of ways. They may be produced by using commercially available portfolio design software. Such programs typically provide a template into which material is placed. More adventurous portfolio designers may use multimedia authoring programs to create their own portfolio template. Electronic portfolios may be authored as connected web pages using HTML programming or with web design authoring software.

Why Design an Electronic Portfolio?

Electronic portfolios can offer some special advantages over traditionally designed versions. These advantages include convenience, interactivity, connectivity, development of technology skills in the course of assembling the portfolio, and demonstration of those skills to supervisors or potential employers.

Portfolios, because they incorporate a large number and wide range of exhibits, can present an organizational challenge (Perone, 1991). The sheer amount of material collected across time, multiplied by the number of performance areas for which material is being collected, can represent a daunting organizational task. The large volume of evidence collected for the portfolio may result in materials that are physically cumbersome, complicating their presentation, evaluation, and interpretation. Transporting and duplicating such materials makes sharing them with others a tedious process. Storing and managing portfolio materials is a concern shared by many educators interested in developing portfolios (Lankes, 1995).

Electronic portfolios represent a medium that can store and organize substantial amounts of material. Video segments, digital photographs, textual material, audio files, and scanned materials, which might have required significant storage space in traditional formats, may now be placed onto a single CD, disk, or online presentation. Electronic portfolios also can be easily duplicated so that copies of the originals may be shared with others.

Organized in a traditional manner (such as three-ring binders or accordion files), portfolios invite linear thinking regarding the collection and presentation of performance evidence and the interpretation of that evidence. Traditional portfolio devices often present evidence in domains or by categories. Important connections between pieces of evidence may be obscured by relatively rigid categorical systems for storage and presentation. Many electronic portfolios allow the designer to connect portfolio entries to each other. The result can be an interactive document with entries meaningfully connected. For example, a lesson plan might be scanned into the electronic portfolio. On that scanned lesson plan the teacher might place a button next to the description of a particularly effective activity. Clicking the button would open up a short video of the activity being conducted during the lesson. Another button on the scanned lesson plan might open multiple windows showing student work produced during the lesson. In the electronic portfolio, these pieces of evidence are connected to strengthen the viewer's understanding of the lesson.

The process of designing an electronic portfolio offers opportunities to develop and refine important technology skills. There may be special value in mastering technology in the process of constructing an electronic portfolio. When technology experiences are placed into the context of valued activities, the acquisition of these skills occurs more meaningfully. As Watts (1997) has observed, technology becomes a catalyst because "in the struggle to master its use, we have, by necessity, become learners" (p. 30). Building an electronic portfolio requires acquiring skill in the use of a variety of types of hardware (scanners, digital cameras, video equipment, and computers) and software (image manipulation programs, video editing and compression utilities, and multimedia authoring). Technology competencies such as these can contribute to increased instructional effectiveness.

How Do I Create an Electronic Portfolio?

Just as is true with traditional portfolio design, careful planning is the key to building a high-quality electronic portfolio. It is important to recognize that the quality of any portfolio, whether electronic or traditional in format, is determined primarily by the decisions made about content and the reflection on that content. The guidelines and principles governing portfolio content and reflection presented in Chapters 4 through 7 apply to electronic formats just as they do to building a traditional portfolio.

Whether the electronic portfolio is being designed by a preservice teacher as a university requirement, by a teacher as a resume for employment purposes, by a beginning teacher as a licensure requirement, or by an experienced teacher seeking an alternative to traditional performance evaluation or pursuing national board certification, similar decisions will guide the design process. There are three basic design options for the electronic portfolio. The portfolio may be created using electronic portfolio software, multimedia software, or web page design software. The option selected for an electronic portfolio depends upon the content to be placed into the portfolio, the uses envisioned for the portfolio, and the audiences expected to view the portfolio.

ELECTRONIC PORTFOLIO SOFTWARE

A number of programs on the market are designed to provide templates for creating an electronic portfolio. Many of these programs are designed to allow teachers to create electronic portfolios with their students. Most, however, may be used to create professional portfolios as well. This software review includes programs designed specifically for professional or pre-professional portfolio design (*The Teacher's Portfolio*), for the design of portfolios for professionals, pre-professionals, and students (*Scholastic Electronic Portfolio*), and programs limited to use in developing student portfolios (*The Portfolio Assessment Kit*). The final software category is included because electronic portfolios developed by students or on students' work may represent especially powerful evidence of teaching effectiveness.

These programs vary considerably with regard to design features. Consider carefully what the electronic portfolio should look like and select the program that will produce the desired style.

FIGURE 9-1 Electronic Portfolio Screen with Timeline Design. Contributed by Debbie Metcalf, a nationally board-certified teacher who is the teacher-in-residence in the Department of Special Education at East Carolina University.

- *Scholastic Electronic Portfolio* (Scholastic, Inc.) is one of the more flexible and powerful programs available. This software allows the user to create a variety of portfolio designs including text, timeline (see Figure 9-1), illustrated, picture (see Figure 9-2), sound, slide show, video, and launch views. Material from any of these views may be linked to any other material in the portfolio using hot-linked text and buttons. In Figure 9-3, a teacher has developed a portfolio for national board certification using *Scholastic Electronic Portfolio* software. The portfolio opens to a window that presents a button with introductory information and five buttons, one for each of the national board propositions. In Figure 9-4, the button labeled Proposition 2 has been clicked and a window has opened to display a detailed narrative describing this teacher's performance relative to this proposition. In this scrolling text window, selected words, phrases, and sentences have been hot-linked to video, digital photographs, text files, sound files, and scanned material. In Figure 9-5, the phrase "weaving mats for our Kwanzaa celebration" has been clicked and a digital photograph of a student's work on this activity is displayed. The software is packaged with a detailed manual and a CD containing 11 model portfolios illustrating the variety of designs possible. Unfortunately, this program is available only for Macintosh. The large number of design options left in the user's control require that some time be spent mastering the program. A tutorial is provided.
- *The Portfolio Assessment Toolkit* (Forest Technologies) is a multimedia electronic portfolio program that includes three customizable portfolios (Primary, Intermediate, and Secondary) that, according to the authors, are adaptable for students and adults of all ages. The software is a

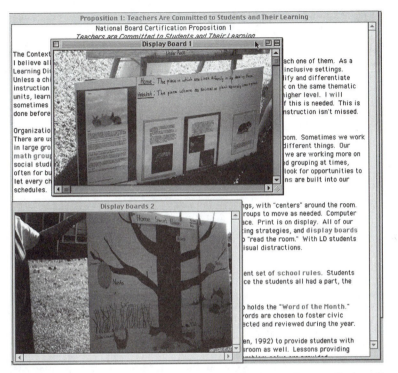

FIGURE 9-2   Screen from Electronic Portfolio Picture Design Option. Contributed by Debbie Metcalf, a nationally board-certified teacher who is the teacher-in-residence in the Department of Special Education at East Carolina University.

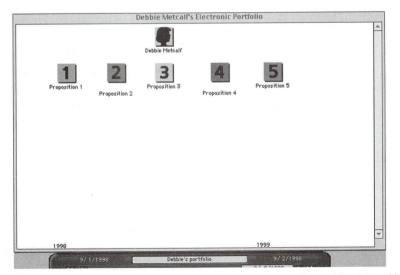

FIGURE 9-3   Sample Electronic Portfolio. Contributed by Debbie Metcalf, a nationally board-certified teacher who is the teacher-in-residence in the Department of Special Education at East Carolina University.

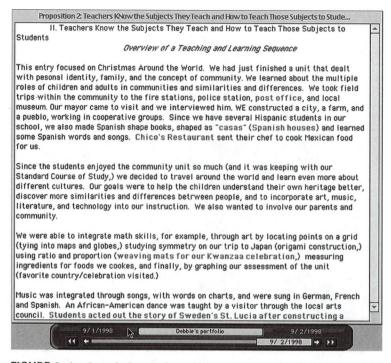

Proposition 2: Teachers KNow the Subjects They Teach and How to Teach Those Subjects to Stude...

II. Teachers Know the Subjects They Teach and How to Teach Those Subjects to Students

Overview of a Teaching and Learning Sequence

This entry focused on Christmas Around the World. We had just finished a unit that dealt with pesonal identity, family, and the concept of community. We learned about the multiple roles of children and adults in communities and similarities and differences. We took field trips within the community to the fire stations, police station, post office, and local museum. Our mayor came to visit and we interviewed him. WE constructed a city, a farm, and a pueblo, working in cooperative groups. Since we have several Hispanic students in our school, we also made Spanish shape books, shaped as "casas" (Spanish houses) and learned some Spanish words and songs. Chico's Restaurant sent their chef to cook Mexican food for us.

Since the students enjoyed the community unit so much (and it was keeping with our Standard Course of Study,) we decided to travel around the world and learn even more about different cultures. Our goals were to help the children understand their own heritage better, discover more similarities and differences betrween people, and to incorporate art, music, literature, and technology into our instruction. We also wanted to involve our parents and community.

We were able to integrate math skills, for example, through art by locating points on a grid (tying into maps and globes,) studying symmetry on our trip to Japan (origami construction,) using ratio and proportion (weaving mats for our Kwanzaa celebration,) measuring ingredients for foods we cookes, and finally, by graphing our assessment of the unit (favorite country/celebration visited.)

Music was integrated through songs, with words on charts, and were sung in German, French and Spanish. An African-American dance was taught by a visitor through the local arts council. Students acted out the story of Sweden's St. Lucia after constructing a

9/1/1998   Debbie's portfolio   9/2/1998

9/ 2/1998

FIGURE 9-4   Sample Screen from Electronic Portfolio. Contributed by Debbie Metcalf, a nationally board-certified teacher who is the teacher-in-residence in the Department of Special Education at East Carolina University.

companion to *HyperStudio.* The program contains 40 ready-made cards to choose from to create and customize the portfolio. Goals can be linked to specific projects, scanned materials, and photographs. A built-in sound recorder feature allows audio reflection. The publisher claims that *The Portfolio Assessment Toolkit* is the only portfolio program that can be moved from Macintosh to Windows with no conversion necessary.

- *The Portfolio Assessment Kit* (Super School Software) provides a collection of programs that may be used to document student work across time. The software contains a family portfolio, a student journal, a recording studio to create and play back multimedia files, My School Work where scanned work is stored and presented, I'm a Happy Writer Portfolio where students employ writing to build skills, Portfolio Conference for notes on parent/teacher conferences, Student Profile where cumulative records are kept, and other components. This multifunctional program is designed primarily to create student portfolios at the elementary level and has limited direct value in the design of professional portfolios.
- *The Portfolio Builder for PowerPoint* (Visions-Technology in Education) is a companion product for PowerPoint users that provides elementary, middle school, secondary, and adult templates for constructing a

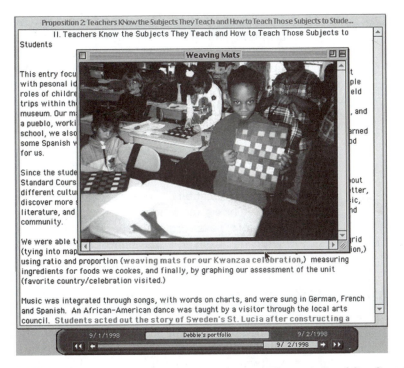

FIGURE 9-5   Sample of Connected Evidence in Electronic Portfolio. Contributed by Debbie Metcalf, a nationally board-certified teacher who is the teacher-in-residence in the Department of Special Education at East Carolina University.

portfolio. Graphics, sound, video, and text may be combined to create a multimedia portfolio. The portfolio created with *The Portfolio Builder* may be published to the Internet. The kit contains student and teacher tutorials, sample products, and the PowerPoint Viewer, which allows portfolios to be played on computers without PowerPoint. This program is available for both Windows and Macintosh platforms.

- *The Teacher's Portfolio* (Aurbach & Associates) is a Macintosh software package that can be used by teachers to create and maintain a professional portfolio, by university personnel to perform portfolio-based evaluation of preservice teachers (using INTASC or other standards), and by administrators to perform portfolio-based evaluation of inservice teachers (using INTASC or other standards). *The Teacher's Portfolio* provides a framework for displaying work in multimedia formats, including sound, graphics, video, text, and computer exhibits. Each portfolio exhibit has specific places for describing the piece, for self-reflection, and for evaluation by the portfolio owner, a supervisor, and a "visitor." A separate Notes section provides room for additional comments or dialog between profile developers and their supervisors or evaluators.

  The Teacher's Portfolio ships with descriptors based on INTASC standards for new teachers and additional descriptors devised by an advisory board of university professors and school professionals. You may use these descriptors, modify them, or discard them and add your own based on local teaching standards or university requirements. The program has room for 10 separate domains (Command of Subject Matter, Knowledge of Pedagogy, Curriculum and Planning, Instructional Strategies, Classroom Management, Diverse Learners, Teacher as Communicator, Teacher as Evaluator, Reflective Practitioner, and Learning Communities) and two journal cards (one for the portfolio owner and one for the supervisor or evaluator). Additionally, *The Teacher's Portfolio* provides a place for teachers to chronicle personal information (address, phone, photo, etc.), professional goals, educational philosophy, experience, development activities, competencies, and academic record. The program prints reports and each portfolio is password protected. Demo versions of the program may be downloaded from *http://www.aurbach.com/*.

MULTIMEDIA AUTHORING SOFTWARE

- *HyperStudio 3.1* is probably the single best choice for authoring one's own portfolio framework. It is the most widely used multimedia authoring software in the educational arena. The user may create connected series of cards with sound, video, text, scanned images, digital photographs, and combinations of the formats. Portfolios created with *HyperStudio* may be placed online, saved to CD, and viewed across platforms.
- *Astound 6.0* is a multimedia authoring program designed to support interactive presentations. *PowerPoint* slides may be imported into *Astound* portfolios and these portfolios may be exported to web pages.

WEB PAGE DESIGN SOFTWARE

With the growing number of people interested in designing their own personal and business web pages has come a large body of easy-to-use web page design software. These software packages typically require little or no programming knowledge. These programs may be used to create an electronic portfolio and place that portfolio online as a series of connected pages. A number of programs currently on the market lend themselves to portfolio design. These include:

- *Adobe PageMill 3.0* (Adobe Systems, Inc.)
- *Microsoft FrontPage 2000* (Microsoft Corp.)
- *Macromedia Dreamweaver 2* (Macromedia, Inc.)

- *Claris Home Page 2* (Claris Corp.)
- *Netscape Composer* (Netscape Communications Corp.)

SELECTING SOFTWARE

A number of issues should be addressed in selecting portfolio design software. These include the portfolio author's technological expertise, the portfolio design desired, and the projected audiences for the portfolio.

First, portfolio developers should consider carefully their level of technological competence. Those with less technological expertise may wish to consider using electronic portfolio software that provides a template. These programs demand no real authoring skill. Those with more advanced technological competence may elect to use multimedia authoring programs and/or web design software.

The use of electronic portfolio software packages that provide templates simplifies the design process but does so at the expense of some design originality. This may be a desirable trade-off for the less experienced author. For those with more advanced skills and experience, multimedia packages offer greater control over the design of the electronic portfolio and allow developers to create unique portfolios.

Developers should consider the audience(s) for their portfolio. Who will view the portfolio, under what circumstances, and for what purposes? Placing one's portfolio online clearly offers access to the widest possible audience. Placing the portfolio on CD results in a portable portfolio, but one that must be delivered to the viewer. Creating an electronic portfolio with extensive multimedia content requires that the viewer have access to a computer system capable of supporting the multimedia files.

HARDWARE CONSIDERATIONS

The collection and processing of entries for an electronic portfolio involve using a variety of types of hardware. Typically, a fully equipped electronic portfolio workstation will include the following:

- **Computer.** Building an electronic portfolio will require access to a personal computer system with adequate memory (RAM) and processing speed to support the use of multimedia software. An AV computer system with video-in-and-out capabilities will be necessary.
- **Scanner.** Scanners have become almost as common as printers. Many are available for under $100 (Grotta & Grotta, 1999). A key feature to consider in the selection of a flatbed scanner is image resolution, expressed as dots-per-inch (dpi). An optical resolution of 600 × 1200 dpi should be a minimum requirement. *PC Magazine* (Yang, 1999) tested 20

scanners all costing less than $500 and found a majority produced excellent image quality. Interestingly, the scanner rated highest on the color photo criteria cost only $80.

- **Digital camera.** A digital camera records images using digital image sensors rather than film. Images captured with a digital camera may be exported directly to a computer, manipulated and edited, and placed into an electronic portfolio. Digital cameras are available at a variety of prices with an equivalent variety of features. For under $250, expect resolutions of only 640 × 480 and only the most basic features. Digital cameras in the $300-plus price range typically provide greater image resolution (1024 × 768 and higher), zoom lenses, and built-in LCD panels. The LCD panel allows users to view the image just captured and choose to discard or save it. The ability to confirm immediately that the image captured is the image needed for the portfolio can be of particular value in photographing fluid classroom events.

- **Video camera.** Most teachers are familiar with this technology. Media centers in most schools are equipped with a video camera that meets all the requirements for capturing video for an electronic portfolio. Depending upon the computer system and video camera used, it may be possible to capture video directly to the computer. In other cases it may be necessary to transfer the video from tape to the computer using a videocassette recorder (VCR). In either case, software is available that will allow image editing (e.g., *Adobe Premier*) and video compression (e.g., *Media Cleaner Pro*). Compressing video is a process that results in video segments requiring much less space to store and run than uncompressed versions.

CONCERNS ASSOCIATED WITH DESIGNING AN ELECTRONIC PORTFOLIO

Portfolio developers must consider a number of issues before deciding to design an electronic portfolio. As exciting and promising as this emerging technology may be, some barriers prevent its widespread use.

Not all electronic portfolios can be viewed on all computer platforms. Some electronic portfolio software is platform specific. Some portfolio viewers may use computer systems not capable of supporting the multimedia content of electronic portfolios. While it seems likely that this issue will become less significant as more people have and use multimedia-capable computer systems, it is at the present time a legitimate concern.

Designing an electronic portfolio may require substantial time and effort devoted to mastering the requisite technologies. Portfolio developers who have little experience with the hardware and software necessary to develop an electronic portfolio and who have little time to devote to mastering these technologies may find a traditional format more efficient. It seems likely that this will become less an issue as more professionals feel comfortable with technology.

Designing an electronic portfolio requires access to a variety of hardware and software. While most schools have these technologies on hand, many individuals may not. Even in school settings, the absence of enough equipment to assure quick and easy access may be an issue complicating electronic portfolio design and frustrating portfolio developers.

There is the possibility that developers and/or viewers of electronic portfolios may find themselves focusing on the design and presentation technologies rather than on the content of the portfolio. Electronic portfolios have value only to the extent that the content is carefully chosen, effectively organized, and rationally interpreted. Placing a poor portfolio into electronic format does not improve the quality of its content.

CLOSING THOUGHTS

Electronic portfolios represent a powerful and innovative medium for the development and presentation of teaching portfolios. The hardware and software required for building electronic portfolios are commonly available in most school and university settings. Prospective and current teachers should possess the technological skills necessary for using the hardware and software. Portfolios are becoming a more common means for documenting and presenting evidence of teaching competence. In the future, the electronic portfolio may become the preferred means for designing, constructing, storing, transporting, and presenting teaching portfolios.

REFERENCES

Adobe PageMill 3.0 [Computer software]. (1999). San Jose, CA: Adobe Systems, Inc.

Claris Home Page 2 [Computer software]. (1999). Santa Clara, CA: Claris Corp.

Grotta, D., & Grotta, S. W. (1999). Scanning made simple [Online]. *PC Magazine.* Available: http://www.zdnet.com/pcmag/stories/reviews/0,6755,410278,00.html.

Lankes, A. M. (1995). Electronic portfolios: A new idea in assessment [Online]. *ERIC Digest, 95*, 9, 1–4. Abstract From: Clearinghouse on Information & Technology: EDO-IR-95-9. Available: http://ericir.syr.edu/ithome/digests/portfolio.html.

Macromedia Dreamweaver 2 [Computer software]. (1999). San Francisco, CA: Macromedia, Inc.

Microsoft FrontPage 2000 [Computer software]. (1999). Redmond, WA: Microsoft Corp.

Netscape Composer [Computer software]. (1999). Mountain View, CA: Netscape Communications Corp.

Perone, V. (Ed.). (1991). *Expanding student assessment.* Alexandria, VA: Association of Supervision and Curriculum Development.

The Scholastic Electronic Portfolio [Computer software]. (1995). New York: Scholastic, Inc.

Watts, M. M. (1997). Technology as catalyst. *Educational Perspectives: Journal of the College of Education/University of Hawaii at Manoa, 31*(2), 28–31.

Yang, S. J. (1999). Performance tests: Flatbed scanners [Online]. *PC Magazine.* Available: http://www.zdnet.com/pcmag/stories/reviews/0,6755,410416,00.html.

APPENDIX

A

Reflection Analyses for Chapter 3

AUTHOR'S ANALYSIS FOR REFLECTION ONE

Score: ++ This reflection is excellent. It gives an excellent description, analysis, and planning for future teaching. The description is clear. The audience is a university professor, and the student writes in first person, appropriate for a self-reflection. In the analysis section, the student honestly looks at her strengths and weaknesses in relation to planning and delivering this lesson. The analysis is the strongest part of the reflection.

AUTHOR'S ANALYSIS FOR REFLECTION TWO

Score: + This reflection is well done. It is clearly written and gives a good description and analysis of the lesson. In addition, planning for future teaching was highlighted. In comparison to the first reflection in Chapter 3, this example does not give the extent of detail or the depth of analysis but meets all of the criteria appropriate for reflection.

AUTHOR'S ANALYSIS FOR REFLECTION THREE

Score: +/− The portfolio developer wrote a mediocre description (sometimes off the subject), but wrote a good analysis and did a good job on future impact. The description did not contain enough details for a reader to form an accurate picture of the evidence. In addition, the writing is not clear and there are many grammatical and spelling errors that cloud the reading of the reflection. A peer reader would have been helpful in this case.

North Carolina's Performance-Based Licensure Model for Teachers

Performance-Based
Licensure
1998-99

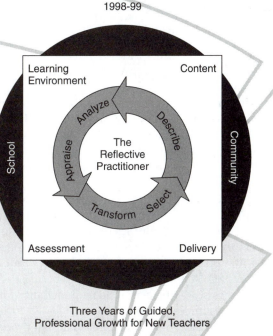

Three Years of Guided,
Professional Growth for New Teachers

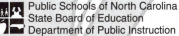 Public Schools of North Carolina
State Board of Education
Department of Public Instruction

Used by permission of Public Schools of North Carolina, State Board of Education, Department of Public Instruction

ACTIVITY #1 DEMONSTRATING YOUR CONTENT KNOWLEDGE AND YOUR ABILITY TO TEACH IT

Standards to be Addressed: 1, 2, 4, 6, 7, 8

Required Components:

Coordinated Set of Evidence consisting of:

- Unit Plan and Goals (labeled clearly)
- 5 Contiguous Lesson Plans (with dates)
- Related Student Work and Assessment/Test Data
- Analysis of Student Achievement Data
- Video for Activity 1
- Video Information Sheet
- Reflection

Optional:

Related Evidence/Artifacts

In this activity the candidate is expected to demonstrate that s/he:

- has an understanding of the central concepts of his/her discipline.
- uses explanations and representations that link curriculum to *prior* learning.
- uses interdisciplinary approaches to teaching and learning.
- uses methods of inquiry that are central to the discipline.
- provides opportunities for students to assume responsibility for and be actively engaged in their learning.
- encourages student reflection on prior knowledge and its connection to new information.
- accesses student thinking as a basis for instructional activities through group/individual interaction and written work (listening, encouraging discussion, eliciting samples of student thinking orally and in writing).
- selects and uses multiple teaching and learning strategies (a variety of presentations/explanations) to encourage students in critical thinking and problem solving.
- encourages students to assume responsibility for identifying and using learning resources.
- assumes different roles in the instructional process (instructor, facilitator, coach, audience) to accommodate content, purpose, and learner needs.
- models effective communication strategies in conveying ideas and information and when asking questions (e.g., monitoring the effects of messages; restating ideas and drawing connections; using visual, aural, and kinesthetic cues; being sensitive to nonverbal cues, both given and received).

- provides support for learner expression in speaking, writing, and other media.
- uses a variety of media communication tools to enrich learning opportunities.
- develops plans that are appropriate for curriculum goals and are based on effective instruction.
- adjusts plans to respond to unanticipated sources of input and/or student needs.
- develops short- and long-range plans.
- selects, constructs, and uses assessment strategies appropriate to the learning outcomes.
- uses a variety of informal and formal strategies to determine student progress and to adjust instruction (e.g., standardized test data, peer and student self-assessment, informal assessments such as observations, surveys, interviews, student work, performance tasks, portfolios, and teacher-made tests).
- evaluates the effects of class activities on individuals and on groups through observation of classroom interaction, questioning, and analysis of student work.

Directions to the Candidate:

1. Select a concept from the *North Carolina Standard Course of Study* or other state-adopted curriculum documents appropriate to your field.
2. Collect and compile the required evidence related to that concept and any additional evidence you want to use to support the standards addressed.
3. Describe how you taught this concept in terms of instructional planning, resources, delivery, and assessment.
4. Address how your assessment/test data affected your instructional planning and delivery.
5. Use the questions on the following page to guide your reflection.

WRITING THE REFLECTION

Below are the guiding questions for the required reflection for Activity 1. In an effort to tailor your product to your style, you may choose to follow the questions as exactly as they are posed, use them strictly as an outline for topics which need to be covered as you reflect, or use the indicators from the INTASC Standards addressed in Activity 1 for writing your reflection. Note: The questions come directly from those indicators. Again, choose your evidence/artifacts carefully; they should show your development as a professional as well as the impact on your students. Be sure that your reflection references the evidence/artifacts that you have included with Activity 1.

Select

1. What concept are you addressing from your content area?
2. Why did you decide to address this concept?
3. How does this concept relate to your students' age group?

Describe

1. Briefly describe the demographics of your class(es). Include a breakdown by gender, race, grade levels, etc. Include a description of any particular student needs in the classroom.
2. What unique student characteristics did you consider in planning the lessons?
3. What diverse student perspectives did you consider in planning the lessons?
4. What kind of assessment of student learning and development did you use prior to planning the lesson(s)? How did you identify exceptional learning needs?
5. Did the school (district) have appropriate resources/materials for this unit? What materials/resources did you choose to use? Include any media tools you incorporated.
6. What resources or services did you incorporate in this unit?
7. What kinds of multiple teaching strategies did you choose to incorporate in your lesson(s)?
8. What roles (coach, audience, facilitator, etc.) did you play to encourage student learning?
9. What strategies did you use to assess student learning? What assessments are required?
10. How did you maintain records of student work and performance?

Analyze

1. How did your assessment of prior student learning and development influence the lesson design?
2. How did the unique characteristics (including exceptional learning needs) of your students impact your planning for the unit?
3. How did you allow students to use different performance modes (writing, speaking, behaving, etc.)?
4. How did you link your students' experiences with the events and experiences of this lesson(s)?
5. How did your plan(s) allow modification for unanticipated sources of input or unanticipated student needs?
6. How did you evaluate the available resources/materials for inclusion in the lesson(s)?
7. Why did you select the teaching and assessment strategies you incorporated in the lesson?

8. How did you:
   - demonstrate a link to students' prior learning?
   - show the use of a variety of informal and formal assessment strategies to inform choices and adjust instruction.
   - show that you have addressed long- and short-range planning based on your knowledge of the subject matter, students, community, and curriculum goals?
9. How does the video show your support for learner expression?
10. How have you taken gender and culture into account in your communication with students?

Appraise

1. What new learning resulted from the activity(ies) conducted for you and your students?[9]
2. How did the use of selected multiple teaching strategies increase your students' opportunities to engage in critical thinking and problem-solving activities?
3. How effectively were you able to use the available resources/materials for this lesson?
4. Which media communication tools have been most and least effective in your classroom?
5. How successful was the lesson? What was most effective? Least effective?

Transform

1. What did you learn from planning the lesson?
2. How did you adjust instruction as a result of assessment of student learning?
3. In teaching this unit or a similar unit in the future, how will this experience influence your choice of instructional and assessment techniques?
4. What did you learn from the selection of multiple teaching strategies?

ACTIVITY #2 EXAMINING THE SCHOOL-COMMUNITY LINK: YOUR ROLE IN A LEARNING COMMUNITY

Standard to be Addressed: 10
Required Components:

- Professional Contribution Log
- Parent/Guardian Communication Log
- Parent Survey(s) Example and Summary
- Reflection

Optional:

Related evidence/artifacts
In this activity the candidate is expected to demonstrate that s/he:

- participates in collegial activities designed to make the entire school a productive learning environment.
- links with counselors, teachers of other classes and activities within the school, professionals in community agencies, and others in the community to support students' learning and well-being.
- seeks to establish cooperative partnerships with parents/guardians to support student learning.
- advocates for students.

Directions to Candidate:

1. Collect and compile the required evidence as well as any additional evidence you want to use to support the standard addressed.
2. Create a parent survey or use the sample parent survey in the Tool Kit.
3. Summarize the findings of your parent survey. You will need to create a form that details the number of responses to each question as well as provides the anecdotal comments from the parents surveyed. If you create your own survey, include a copy.
4. Use the questions on the following page to guide your reflection.

WRITING THE REFLECTION

Below are the guiding questions for the required reflection for Activity 2. In an effort to tailor your product to your style, you may choose to follow the questions as exactly as they are posed. Use them strictly as an outline for topics which need to be covered as you reflect, or use the indicators from INTASC Standard 10 addressed in Activity 2 for writing your reflection. Note: The questions come directly from those indicators. Again, choose your evidence/artifacts carefully; they should show your development as a professional as well as the impact on your students. Be sure that your reflection references the evidence/artifacts that you have included with Activity 2.

Select

1. How do the evidence/artifacts you have selected address Standard 10?

Describe

1. In what collegial activities did you participate to make the entire school a productive learning environment?
2. What partnerships did you establish with the parents/guardians of your students?

3. What interactions did you maintain with counselors, other teachers, community agencies, and others to support students' well-being?

Analyze

1. How and for what reasons did you establish partnerships with parents/guardians? Refer to the evidence presented in your product.
2. How does the evidence presented show your advocacy for students?
3. How did the activities presented allow you to participate in making the entire school a productive learning environment?
4. Based on the information from your parent surveys, what are some positive and negative steps that you have taken this year related to parent and student contact?

Appraise

1. What benefits have derived from the partnerships you established with parents, guardians, and others in the school community?

Transform

1. Based on your experiences, what strategies will you use in the future to establish your role as a learner/advocate in the school community?

ACTIVITY #3 FOCUSING ON THE CLASSROOM CLIMATE

Standard to be Addressed: 5

Required Components:

- Classroom Management Plan
- Comparison of Discipline Rates
- Video for Activity 3
- Video Information Sheet
- Reflection

Optional:

Related evidence/artifacts
In this activity the candidate is expected to demonstrate that s/he:

- encourages clear procedures and expectations that ensure students assume responsibility for themselves and others, work collaboratively and independently, and engage in purposeful learning activities.
- engages students by relating lessons to students' personal interests, allowing students to have choices in their learning, and leading students to ask questions and solve problems that are meaningful to them.

- organizes, allocates, and manages time, space, and activities in a way that is conducive to learning.
- organizes, prepares students for, and monitors independent and group work that allows for full and varied participation of all individuals.
- analyzes classroom environment and interactions and makes adjustments to enhance social relationships, student motivation/engagement, and productive work.

Directions to Candidate:

1. Include a copy of your classroom management plan that is clearly labeled.
2. Collect and compile evidence/artifacts you want to use to support Standard 5.
3. Summarize your student surveys, if you wish.
4. Use the questions on the following section to guide your reflection.

WRITING THE REFLECTION

Below are the guiding questions for the required reflection for Activity 3. In an effort to tailor your product to your style, you may choose to follow the questions as exactly as they are posed, use them strictly as an outline for topics which need to be covered as you reflect, or use the indicators from INTASC Standard 5 addressed in Activity 3 for writing your reflection. Note: The questions come directly from those indicators. Again, choose your evidence/artifacts carefully; they should show your development as a professional as well as the impact on your students. Be sure that your reflection references the evidence/artifacts that you have included with Activity 3.

Select

1. What evidence/artifacts have you selected to address Standard 5?

Describe

1. Describe your classroom management plan. What guidelines did you use to develop this plan?
2. Describe a student who was a discipline challenge during the year. In reflecting on the situation, what specific actions did you take that were productive? What specific actions did you take that were unproductive?
3. What interactions did you maintain with counselors, other teachers, community agencies, and others to support students' well-being?

Analyze

1. Describe three adjustments in your classroom environment that you have made to ensure students are engaged in learning rather than in inappropriate behavior.

2. How do you manage time, space, and activities to ensure students are actively engaged in learning?
3. When did you develop your classroom management plan? What have you done to implement your management plan? Have you modified it? If so, how?
4. How do you provide relevance and choice to engage students in their own learning?

Appraise

1. Explain how the evidence presented (management plan, video, etc.) shows that you have established clear procedures and expectations that students assume responsibility for themselves and others, work collaboratively and independently, and engage in purposeful learning activities.

Transform

1. What kind of adjustments have you made to your management plan and what was the impact of those changes?
2. Based on your experiences, what changes might you make in your management plan in the future?

ACTIVITY #4 ADDRESSING STUDENTS' UNIQUE LEARNING NEEDS

Standards to be Addressed: 2, 3, 8, 10
Required Components:

- 2 Case Studies
- Related Student Work
- Student Test/Assessment Data
- Video for Activity 4
- Video Information Sheet
- Reflection

Optional:

Related evidence/artifacts
In this activity the candidate is expected to demonstrate that s/he:

- evaluates student performance to design instruction appropriate for social, cognitive, and emotional development.
- designs instruction appropriate to students' stages of development, learning styles, strengths, and needs.
- creates relevance for students by linking with their prior experiences.

- selects approaches that provide opportunities for different performance modes.
- accesses appropriate services or resources to meet exceptional learning needs.
- adjusts instruction to accommodate the learning differences or needs of students (time and circumstance of work, tasks assigned, communication, and response modes).
- plans lessons and activities to address variations in learning styles and performance modes, multiple developmental levels of diverse learners, and problem solving and exploration.
- uses knowledge of different cultural contexts within the community (socioeconomic, ethnic, cultural) and connects with the learner through types of interaction and assignments.
- creates a learning community that respects individual differences.
- maintains useful records of student work and performance and can communicate student progress knowledgeably and responsibly.
- links with counselors, teachers of other classes and activities within the school, professionals in community agencies, and others in the community to support students' learning and well-being.

Directions to Candidate:

1. From the case studies that you have done during the school term (quarter, semester, year—whatever your particular length of student interaction is), choose two students with differing physical, social, emotional, and intellectual characteristics which have impacted their learning. In choosing students, remember that you need to show student growth as facilitated by your actions/interactions.
2. Write case studies of these two students which include, but are not limited to: the particular learning problems the students have; the instructional strategies which you have used and/or modified to improve their learning; the changes you have noted in the students since you began your interactions; other factors which have impacted their learning and the level of success of your interventions; and the types of records you have kept related to these students. Your case studies should be no more than one page each.
3. Provide examples of modified student work related to the coordinated set of lesson plans in Activity 1 for the students in the case studies as well as other students with particular needs.
4. Collect and compile any additional evidence you want to use to support the standards addressed.
5. Realize that some of the questions in the reflection will refer to the lesson plans that you included in Activity 1.
6. Summarize student surveys, if you wish.
7. Use the questions on the following page to guide your reflection.

WRITING THE REFLECTION

Below are the guiding questions for the required reflection for Activity 4. In an effort to tailor your product to your style, you may choose to follow the questions as exactly as they are posed; use them strictly as an outline for topics which need to be covered as you reflect; or use the indicators from the INTASC Standards addressed in Activity 4 for writing your reflection. Note: The questions come directly from those indicators. Again, choose your evidence/artifacts carefully; they should show your development as a professional as well as the impact on your students. Be sure that your reflection references the evidence/artifacts that you have included with Activity 4.

Select

1. What evidence/artifacts have you selected to address the INTASC Standards?

Describe

1. What are the unique characteristics that distinguish these students from others (learning styles, prior experiences, exceptional needs, background, etc.)?
2. What steps did you take to assess the needs of these students?
3. With whom and in what ways did you communicate the needs and progress of these students?
4. From whom and in what ways did you solicit information about the students' experiences, learning behaviors, needs, and progress?

Analyze

1. How did your assessment of the characteristics and needs of these students impact your planning instruction and interactions with them?
2. As you implemented your lesson plans, what adjustments did you make to accommodate the learning differences or needs for these students as well as the variety of students in your whole class? In other words, how did you meet all of your students' needs?
3. What evidence/artifacts have you provided which show you meeting the needs of a variety of students?
4. How did the cultural context of these students influence your planning for them and your interactions with them?
5. How did you incorporate cultural knowledge into your lesson plans?
6. How did you select and incorporate special resources or services for these students?

Appraise

1. What interventions/interactions with these students were productive in improving student learning/behavior?

2. What interventions/interactions with these students were unproductive in improving student learning/behavior?
3. What sources of information and assistance were most helpful to you in meeting the unique needs of these students?
4. Were the students identified in your case studies successful this year? Why or why not?

Transform

1. What did you learn from developing the case studies about the diverse nature and needs of students?
2. What new learning on your part will you incorporate in your future teaching?

ACTIVITY #5 APPRAISING YOURSELF AS A PROFESSIONAL

Standard to be Addressed: 9
Required Components:

- Beginning Teacher Individualized Growth Plan
- Self-Administered Interview (clearly labeled)
  Year 1
  Year 2
  Year 3 (if applicable)
- Summative Evaluation
  Year 1
  Year 2
  Year 3 (if applicable)

Reflection (Note: The required reflection from each activity in the product will also be used to assess this activity.)

Optional:

Related evidence/artifacts
The candidate is expected to demonstrate that s/he:

- uses classroom observation, information about students, and research as sources for evaluating the outcomes of teaching and learning and as a basis for experimenting with, reflecting on, and revising practice.
- uses professional literature, colleagues, and other resources (such as professional organizations) to support self-development as a learner and as a teacher.

- consults with professional colleagues within the school and other professional arenas as support for reflection, problem-solving and new ideas, actively sharing experiences, and seeking and giving feedback.

Directions to Candidate:

1. Complete the Beginning Teacher Individualized Growth Plan at the end of year one, year two, and year three if applicable.
2. Collect and compile any additional evidence you want to use to support Standard 9.
3. Include up to three colleagues' surveys, if you wish.

Analysis of Student Work: Assessment

INSTRUCTIONAL CONTEXT

The class represented in the Analysis of Student Work: Assessment section is AP Statistics. It consists of a class of high school seniors, ranging in age from 17 to 18 years old. This class has a broad range of abilities. There are students in my class who have never taken an AP class before and had no idea of the time, effort or thought this class was going to require. I have students who have taken and received credit for 5 or 6 AP classes, who were very well prepared for what they were going to be required to do and who have an interest and desire to learn AP Statistics. Of the 24 students in the class, 10 are identified academically gifted. There is one student who is a single mother, one student with some serious health problems which requires him to miss class frequently, and four students with very serious problems in their home life. The rest of my class primarily comes from middle to upper class backgrounds whose parents are, for the most part, college graduates who are employed at the local university, the hospital (we have a regional medical center and med school), or the local pharmaceutical firm which is our county's biggest non-government employer.

Since statistics at the college level has such a high failure rate, many of my students enrolled in this course to get a background in statistics so they would be prepared for it next year. About 8 of them have no plans to take the AP exam and several who have paid deposits are unsure that they are going to. Having students with different expectations and different goals also presents an instructional challenge. Even though the students are made aware at the beginning of

Permission given by the nationally board-certified teacher who wrote this reflection. (Name withheld)

the year that the goal for this course is preparation for the AP exam, many take the course while not planning to take the exam and do not apply themselves as much as they should. This leads to inattentiveness in the classroom and poorly completed assignments. This has the effect of being carried over to the students who are taking the AP exam and cannot afford to be inattentive in class. It is a challenge to keep them all motivated.

There is also a diversity in their educational background. I have students whose prior math courses consisted of Algebra 1, Geometry and Algebra II, and I have others who are concurrently taking AP Calculus. These differences in educational background make this class a challenge to teach. I try to balance activities which will challenge the more advanced students but at the same time not overwhelm the students with less mathematical background.

PLANNING

Objectives:

This assessment was taken from the unit on linear regression. The students should be able to plot a scattergram of the data, develop the least-squares regression equation, and describe, using the correlation coefficient, the strength of the relationship between the two variables. The students should be able to determine whether a *significant* linear relationship exists and determine, using residuals, the aptness of the linear fit. The students should also be able to demonstrate the use of confidence intervals in regression and correlation models. The students should be able to manually compute all values as well as interpret computer regression output for each of the values as it relates to the context of the problem.

Form and Content:

I used a free response format for this assessment to determine the depth of student knowledge in all of the previous objectives. I did not feel that I would be able to significantly assess their knowledge if I used a multiple choice format. My test was developed by me specifically to evaluate each of the objectives mentioned. The first problem is the regression analysis output from a statistical software program called Minitab©. The students had to find the equation for the least squares line using the output and interpret the slope, in the context of the problem. The students then had to determine if the relationship was significant by performing a hypothesis test on the data. The students had to show their understanding of confidence intervals for slope, for an individual number when the price of oranges is \$8, and for the average number of boxes when the price is \$8. In problem number 2 the students had to show their understanding of scattergrams and graphing the line of best fit. The students also in part c, had to justify why they believed a line to be the best model for the data. In problem number 3 the students had to demonstrate their understanding of the correlation coefficient and the coefficient of determination and interpret their values. The students also in problem 4 then had to demonstrate how outliers affected the slope and correlation coefficient if they are removed from the data set. Problem number 2 part b could be done either with slope or with the correlation coefficient. If the student used the correlation coefficient, p, I gave them extra credit as it was not part of what I taught in the unit but they had the option of reading it on their own.

Mathematical Reasoning:

In each of the problems the students were asked to interpret results, define variables within the context of the situation, justify their reasoning, make conclusions and explain their reasoning. I believe that this shows that the test was designed to elicit significant mathematical reasoning on the part of the students. The test was not designed for students to give answers but to show that they understood and could explain what those numbers signified, not just statistically but in the context of the problem situations.

ANALYSIS OF THREE STUDENT RESPONSES

I chose three students of very different abilities and learning styles for this entry. Holly is an example of a high ability student, Amber is a student of average ability, and Kathleen is a student who tries very hard but does not always grasp the concepts completely. The three show an example of the variety of students I teach in this class and a variety of the types of responses the students give.

Holly

I chose Holly because she is an example of one of my high achieving students. Holly studies very hard and could well be classified as an academic overachiever. She is very grade conscious and will go into a panic attack if she does not achieve an A. I believe this stems from a low self-esteem on Holly's part. She is a quiet, shy and very polite girl. She is also very overweight. Holly presents an instructional challenge in her reaction to her grades. It is very difficult as an instructor who cares about her students to watch Holly break down and leave my room in tears in reaction to a grade. It tends to make me feel guilty and I have to guard myself to grade her tests fairly and with the same standards as the other students. She is never upset with me, just herself, but as a teacher, I feel responsible. It rarely happens that her tests are less than adequate for her standards because she works hard to make sure she does well.

Content Mastery:

I believe Holly's test shows that she mastered the concepts of the unit. Three of the five mistakes she made (1c, d, h) were due to errors in simple arithmetic or in the case of problem 1 part h, looking up the value in the row above the one she needed. Her other two mistakes were more critical. In problem 1 part e, Holly confused the coefficient of determination, r^2, with the correlation coefficient, r. This is a very easy mistake to make for first year statistics students and I believe Holly will not make that same mistake again. In problem number 4, however, Holly showed that she might have some misconceptions about the correlation coefficient or at least in why it will change when the outlier is removed.

Mathematical Reasoning:

Throughout Holly's paper she shows mathematical thinking and reasoning in response to each question. In problem 1, she shows her understanding of the slope of the least squares line in part b and clearly states her conclusion in part c. In problem 2 she justifies why she feels that a line is a good model for the data by her use of residuals. In problem 4 Holly again correctly interprets the slope in the context of the problem and explains how the slope of the line will change if the outlier is removed from the data in part d. Because she can explain and justify and not just find answers, I believe this shows Holly's understanding of the procedures she is performing. The procedures are not the end in themselves but what they mean in the context of each problem. Holly shows that reasoning throughout her paper.

Feedback:

I go over each problem in class when I hand back the test. Holly asked questions about what she got wrong and was able to understand and correct her mistakes. I also told her specifically to practice her arithmetic because even though she understood the concepts clearly she also needs to be able to get the correct answer. I told her that if she was working for a corporation and not just taking statistics as a class, her research and her job would depend on accuracy.

Amber

I chose Amber because she exemplifies my "average" student. Amber is bright but does not study any harder than she has to. She is very pretty and very popular and she also is a talented athlete. For these reasons, Amber tends to put studying third on her list of priorities after sports and socializing. As a learner, Amber tends to be a "cookbook" learner. She wants to have a recipe for doing each problem that she can follow every time having to put in little thought of her own. Because of this, Amber's answers can be very canned. She always wants to know when I am teaching a subject, how I would state my conclusion or justify a response. Her response to a similar prompt on a test will be exactly like I phrased it. It is a challenge for me to get Amber to think on her own and to take risks in her ideas.

In problem number 1, Amber showed some misconceptions in parts g and h in her interpretation of the Minitab© printout. She also was careless in her definition of the slope in part b and did not consider what the values represented. This mistake was very significant because if she had just read what she wrote, I would like to think she would have realized that it was very unrealistic. This shows Amber's reluctance to take a risk. She is more worried about how she is saying it than what she is saying. Amber also shows a gap in her prior knowledge in problem 2 in plotting the least squares line. Plotting lines is a topic that I reviewed but is initially taught in Algebra 1. Amber also had not mastered the concept of residuals as indicated by the blank answer on her paper. She does show in her answer to problem 3 (on notebook paper) that she did master the concept of r and r^2 and hypothesis testing for significant correlation between variables. Problem 4 indicates Amber's misconception about the slope in part b and in part c and she does not read the problem carefully and does not fully answer it.

Mathematical Reasoning:

Amber shows that she is capable of doing the computations. Mathematically, her arithmetic is correct. Her reasoning however, is flawed. Her conclusion to problem 1 part b is wrong even though her understanding of the printout is correct. She rejects the null hypothesis but then concludes she does not have enough evidence to prove her alternative, which she does. She shows significant understanding of r and r^2 with her interpretation to each in problem 3. The flawed reasoning that most concerns me is her interpretations of the slope in problems 1 and 4. She understands what is happening, but she just has her variables turned around. But she should have realized that by her illogical answers. Neither answer makes sense. In problem 1 part b she states "for every box (of oranges sold) there is a $763 increase in price." In problem 4 she states ".0534 is the number of the students enrolled in grades 9-12 for every state." She understood what numbers went in the sentence but displayed no understanding of what they meant or where they went. If she had taken the time to read the sentence, she might have realized her mistake.

Feedback:

Amber needed remediation in 3 areas: understanding and interpreting the slope, graphing lines, and using residuals to justify the linear model. I met with Amber and several other students who needed help with these concepts before school for a few days (as I do cover all tests for students who need extra help). I also keep encouraging Amber to use her own words and she would have better understanding of the material. I also started doing more group projects with this class. I thought Amber and several other students who have the same problem would benefit in working with other students and trying to explain and justify their conclusions to them.

Kathleen

Kathleen is a hard worker but tends to be a low functioning student. I chose her as a representative of the students in my class who struggle with the difficult concepts in statistics. Kathleen regularly comes by for extra help after school, does or at least attempts, all her homework, and still does not make the grades she would like. She signed up for stats because all her friends were in the class. Kathleen is the type of student who pays attention in class and while you are going over the material and discussing it, she can answer any question you ask her. Once she leaves class, she forgets everything she knows. When she comes by for help after school I reteach the lesson again. She might retain 40% of what we have done the second time. I go over homework in class the next day and essentially, as I am doing the problems, go over the concepts again. By the time the unit test comes, Kathleen has had more hours of instruction than anyone in the class and probably studied harder, however, her grade will be one of the lowest in the class. Because of this Kathleen can be a challenge to teach. I have encouraged her to use a tape recorder to help at night while she is doing her homework, but she refuses.

Content Mastery:

Kathleen has missed some essential concepts of the unit. Based on her response to problems 1 and 4, it is apparent that she does not know how to read a computer printout for the information it contains. She could not find the least squares line, define the slope, find the coefficient of determination, or compute the confidence intervals when asked in number 1. In number 4 similarly, she had no understanding of how the values in parts c and d would change if the outlier was removed from them. She also has some gaps in her knowledge hypothesis testing. She understood the majority of the setup of the test in problem 1 part c but in problem 3 part b when asked to do the same type of problem, did not know how to start but wrote down numbers. This kind of inconsistency is typical of Kathleen.

Mathematical Reasoning:

Kathleen's mathematical reasoning can be seen in three places. The first place is problem 1 part c. In this problem, even though she uses the wrong number to calculate her t-value she does understand what the t-value means in terms of her problem and states the correct conclusion based on the answer she got to the problem. I also think problem 3 part a shows her understanding of what r and r^2 mean. Even though she doesn't correctly calculate r^2 she does understand that it represents the variation in the problem. If r^2 was incorrect then r also was incorrect, but she does show that she understands that the values are positively correlated, however she missed the important fact that r should always be values of -1 and 1. Kathleen shows incorrect reasoning in her conclusion to part c of problem 3 because she bases the relationship of the line on the residuals and completely forgets about the information she had drawn in the previous part. The blank responses on her test show her inability to make connections and reason through the problems, with or without the practical knowledge of being able to calculate the correct number.

Feedback:

Kathleen and I covered every problem on her test again after school. We went over mistakes in concepts and discussed how she could improve her score by at least expanding on what things meant, even if she could not get the correct numerical answer. I give her credit for what is right in the response so even if she got the wrong value she could have partial credit for her explanations and justifications.

Reflection

Further Instruction:

After evaluating my students' performance on this test, I felt confident about their understanding of the important concepts of this unit. I learned that, for the most part, they were capable of performing the correct calculations or interpretations of computer generated data for the objectives stated previously for this unit. Furthermore, they showed significant mathematical reasoning in their justifications, conclusions and interpretations of those results.

Holly's paper suggests that she is ready to move on to the next concept. Her mistakes are simple arithmetic which is mainly due to carelessness not a lack of understanding of the concepts. My evidence for this is her responses both in performing the mathematical calculations and in her justifications and conclusions she states. Holly has learned the material presented and has displayed that knowledge with confidence evidenced in all her responses.

Amber's paper suggests that she is also ready to move on to the next concept. Though she does not display the depth of understanding that Holly exhibits, she still clearly has mastered the majority of the concepts. I think Amber needs to spend some time before or after school to review some of the concepts such as the meaning of the slope and her lack of understanding of residual, that she did have difficulty with. Amber and I, along with a few more of her classmates that needed the same type of help, did spend some time before school in remediation.

Kathleen's paper suggests more of a challenge. The majority of my class is ready to move on to the next concept but Kathleen is not. Since Kathleen has been attending regular sessions with me after school, I decided that the best course for her was to remediate the concepts she missed during these one-on-one sessions. The evidence for her lack of understanding of the basic concepts can be seen in the many blank spaces on her test where she really had no understanding of how to attempt the problem.

Evaluation of Assessment:

I thought the test was a good overall picture of the concepts the students should know. It addressed each objective in a clear and precise manner. It allowed me to assess the students' ability to perform the basic calculations by the computational part of each problem. It also allowed me to evaluate their understanding of what these answers represent by their responses to the conclusion or justification part to each problem.

If I use this assessment again, I might try adding some multiple choice problems to give the students a variety of testing formats. I also need to fix the typographical errors in problem 1 where I have fives in the first line instead of gives and I left out part f in labeling the parts to the problem.

APPENDIX C ADDENDUM

A few thoughts about the commentary

The commentary follows the basic process of reflection presented in Chapter 3: description, analysis, and planning. Specific questions asked in the activity are answered. The reflection is well written and is within the page limit required by NBPTS. This candidate has done an excellent job with this commentary. If there are still questions about reflection, reread Chapter 3.

Council of Exceptional Children Standards

The Council for Exceptional Children is the leading professional organization for teachers of children with special needs. This organization has developed Professional Practice Standards. These standards can be used as a framework for developing a professional portfolio.

THE STANDARDS

The standards are divided into five areas: (1) Instructional Responsibilities, (2) Management of Behavior, (3) Support Procedures, (4) Parent Relationships, and (5) Advocacy. Each section has quality indicators that describe and give definition to the area. For example, the area of Instructional Responsibilities is outlined below. For quality indicators for all five areas, refer to www.cec.sped.org.

Area: Instructional Responsibilities

Special education personnel are committed to the application of professional expertise to ensure the provision of quality education for all individuals with exceptionalities. Professionals strive to:

1. Identify and use instructional methods and curricula that are appropriate to their area of professional practice and effective in meeting the individual needs of persons with exceptionalities.
2. Participate in the selection and use of appropriate instructional materials, equipment, supplies, and other resources needed in the effective practice of their profession.
3. Create safe and effective learning environments, which contribute to the fulfillment of needs, stimulation of learning, and self-concept.

4. Maintain class size and case loads that are conducive to meeting the individual needs of individuals with exceptionalities.
5. Use assessment instruments and procedures that do not discriminate against persons with exceptionalities on the basis of race, color, creed, sex, national origin, age, political practices, family or social background, sexual orientation, or exceptionality.
6. Base grading, promotion, graduation, and/or movement out of the program on the individual goals and objectives for individuals with exceptionalities.
7. Provide accurate program data to administrators, colleagues, and parents, based on efficient and objective record keeping practices, for the purpose of decision making.
8. Maintain confidentiality of information except when information is released under specific conditions of written consent and statutory confidentiality requirements.

HOW CAN A PORTFOLIO BE ORGANIZED AROUND THESE STANDARDS?

A portfolio would be organized much like the INTASC examples presented in Chapter 2 or Chapter 6, depending on the purpose. A product or showcase portfolio would be appropriate to develop for these standards.

For a product design, the portfolio could easily be divided into the five areas. Evidence would be placed in each of the areas to support the quality indicators. One reflection could be written per area.

These standards could also be used as a teacher recruitment tool or as an alternative evaluation model. A showcase portfolio could be developed around the five areas for job interviews, including evidence that demonstrates the indicators. Alternative evaluation portfolio developers could use the professional goal framework, choosing an area (or two) as their professional goals. Evidence would document how the goal (area) was being met. This model would be particularly effective as a precursor to the NBPTS process.

APPENDIX E

Canadian Curriculum Standards: Foundation Statements for Science Literacy

Canada is mirroring the United States by creating sets of national standards for various curriculum areas. These standards are being developed across provinces. One of the first areas developed was science literacy. The science literacy standards are based on four foundational statements:

1. Students will develop an understanding of the nature of science and technology, of the relationship between science and technology, and of the social and environmental contexts of science and technology.
2. Students will develop the skills required for scientific and technological inquiry, for solving problems, for communicating scientific ideas and results, for working collaboratively, and for making informed decisions.
3. Students will construct knowledge and understandings of concepts in life science, physical science, and Earth and space science, and apply these understandings.
4. Students will be encouraged to develop attitudes that support the responsible acquisition and application of scientific and technological knowledge to the mutual benefit of self, society, and the environment.

HOW CAN A PORTFOLIO BE ORGANIZED AROUND THESE STANDARDS?

If a teacher wants to show these standards have been met, a product portfolio could be developed with each foundational belief becoming an area or domain.

161

Student work related to learning outcomes would be included. Reflections could focus on how the teacher is meeting the foundational standards.

National Council for Teachers of Mathematics K–12 Standards

The National Council for Teachers of Mathematics was one of the first professional groups to create a set of national standards related to student learning. These ten standards are divided into two areas: (1) mathematical content students should learn, and (2) mathematical processes through which students should acquire and use their mathematical knowledge.

THE STANDARDS

Mathematical content standards include:

1. Number and Operations
2. Patterns, Functions, and Algebra
3. Geometry and Spatial Sense
4. Measurement
5. Data Analysis, Statistics, and Probability

MATHEMATICAL PROCESSES

1. Problem Solving
2. Reasoning and Proof
3. Communication
4. Connections
5. Representation

For each standard, quality indicators are given. For example, Standard One—Number and Operations:

Mathematics instructional programs should foster the development of number and operation sense so that all students:

- Understand numbers, ways of representing numbers, relationships among numbers, and number systems;
- Understand the meaning of operations and how they relate to each other;
- Use computational tools and strategies fluently and estimate appropriately. (National Council for Teachers of Mathematics)

HOW CAN A PORTFOLIO BE ORGANIZED AROUND THESE STANDARDS?

A product portfolio could be developed around the two areas—content and processes. Developers would include evidence for each of the standards (five for each area) recognizing each quality indicator. One might think it would be easier to show standards individually, but this can be difficult, especially since the standards overlap. By dividing it into content and processes, two broad areas, more flexibility is given to the developer. Reflections can be written for each of the two areas.

INDEX